To David and Elizabeth,
who (for mistaken encouragement)
must share the responsibility for this,
with many thanks and warmest regards,

[signature]

ONE'S COMPANY

ONE'S COMPANY

by
Gerald Lynch

MOSAIC PRESS
Oakville - New York - London

CANADIAN CATALOGUING IN PUBLICATION DATA

Lynch, Gerald, 1953-
    One's company

ISBN 0-88962-421-6 (bound) ISBN 0-88962-420-8 (pbk.)

I. Title.

PS8573.Y5305 1989   C813'.54   C89-09763-5
PR9199.3.L9505 1989

Published by MOSAIC PRESS, P.O. Box 1032, Oakville, Ontario, L6J 5E9, Canada. Offices and warehouse at 1252 Speers Road, Units# 1&2, Oakville, Ontario, L6L 5N9, Canada.

Mosaic Press acknowledges the assistance of the Canada Council and the Ontario Arts Council in support of its publishing programme.

Copyright © Gerald Lynch, 1989
Design by Rita Vogel
Typeset by Aztext Electronic Publishing Ltd.
Cover Illustration & Design by Marion Black
Printed and bound in Canada.

ISBN 0-88962-420-8 PAPER   ISBN 0-88962-421-6 CLOTH

MOSAIC PRESS:
In Canada:
        MOSAIC PRESS, 1252 Speers Road, Units# 1&2, Oakville, Ontario L6J 5N9, Canada. P.O. Box 1032, Oakville, Ontario L6J 5E9

In the United States:
        Riverrun Press Inc., 1170 Broadway, Suite 807, New York, N.Y., 10001, U.S.A., distributed by Kampmann & Co., 9 East 40th Street, New York, N.Y., 10016

In the U.K.:
        John Calder (Publishers) Ltd., 18 Brewer Street, London, W1R 4A5, England.

In memory of
Jimmy
(1962-1979)

Acknowledgements

The following stories appeared originally in the following publications:

"One's Company" in *The Capilano Review*
"In Violet Air" in *Prism International*
"Assault Nets Fine" and "Helpmate" in *Canadian Fiction Magazine*
"Rounded with a Sleep" in *Waves*
"Spice Cake" in *The University of Windsor Review*
"Things Coming Together" and "The Lumbs" in
Wascana Review
"Potlatch" in *Descant*
"The Go-Away Game" in *The Dalhousie Review*
"Floating" in *Matrix*
"The Chemical Valley" in *Canadian Author & Bookman*

Contents

One's Company

Here, one neither smiles approvingly nor nods promptingly when you pause. Such encouraging company is but bidingly solicitous. Such company is (if one may be permitted the frank expression) *after* something. You may act so yourself under exacting circumstances of home and work, which is fine and as it should be. But here one neither concurs nor flatters by grunt or grin. One sits silently as you talk. To maintain one's witness to your discourse, you have but to buy one's beer.

Therefore, when details of domesticity or profession steal centre stage, you need suffer no apprehension over their cuing interruption. Here, you can practice blunting your self-obsessiveness in other-referential terms, with no thought whatsoever of actually deferring to the other. You see the utility of such a skill. Yes. Here, you are freed to concentrate solely on such things as your romance, wedding plans, the progress of a pregnancy, the acquisition of language/syntax/grammar, the rewards of your work that surpass material gain, et cetera. You are also at liberty to talk of loneliness, infertility, spiritual frustration.

In fact, you may discover in one's company that such priceless opportunity to talk leads the speaker to various losses, movingly elegiac at best, bathetically nostalgic at . . . Say simply, at other times. This too is fine.

But you are wary yet of one's company. Understanably so, after that little performance. Come, one will feed for a time your appetite for explanations.

One's world can end in a moment—a stroke, a spray of missiles. One counters such consciousness of the apocalyptic moment with the temporal traumas of others, something of a mystical moment with one. To illustrate the principle: you have heard some such oxymoronic equivalent of, "It was only for a short time, but it felt like forever"? Or, "Time flies when you're having a good time." A happy life is experienced as a brief one. Ugliness, pain, horror, these slow the clock. Consider: the maimed, or the congenitally malformed, or the single mother of six who works twelve-hour nights as a prostitute, or those obsessed to illness with nuclear conflagration, the environment, AIDS, or those who suffer multiplying torments of the mind—those souls are living lives at least three times longer than yours. They suffer? Their suffering should be considered, as the old joke has it, with a view to the alternatives: happy and short lives, brief and brave lives, lives of normal duration whose distinguishing features are compromise, disillusionment, cowardice, shame, dishonour, submission, et cetera.

Look here, now. One has felt years of his life slide by as a few nights, as a single night, as a deep dream. At times when passing happy (and chasing still more happiness), one has let his time slip away like a tail down a hole. One came to recognize a universal truth: To pursue happiness is to hurry death. No Zen priest, one became instead the vicar of the vicarious, welcoming your sad talk, dark talk, regretful talk, remorseful talk, resentful talk, your lonely, defeated talk, your continuous talk of discontinuity, your disjointed talk of fragmentation, your disappointed talk of failure. Even your suicidal talk. Should words fail you, one will act as your third person. Thus one elaborates his brief sentence here. Thus one endures.

One has no home, no family, no wife, no job. One's company is, as you may have guessed, one's company. Because one skittishly harbours no personal tales to talk of, he will not obstruct the ascent of your anecdotes to climax. Oh, once upon a time one was wont to reflect and expound on his brief life at length, and brazenly to fashion all manner of meaning between what was, what is, and what shall be. At the omega of time and space, there rested a musing one, the beatified individual, the cannonized ironic. But some time ago one's life-in-story slowly then suddenly gave up its ghost of meaning. One admitted that his self-serving tales had been told before, and better. As a teller of tales, one began to distrust his paling persona. Words soon ceased to have significant reference, or at least the highly moral meaning one thought he'd wanted. Listeners misheard, readers misread, purposely it seemed. So, instead of holding forth in this steaming pisshole, one made of himself a thirsty ear. To make a long story short . . . well, perhaps that's enough.

Here then, one pours instead the foundation of trust for our acquaintance: what one was is of no further interest; what he is he will remain, silently so. To repeat, you have no call to concern yourself about distractions along these lines. Here, you may speak of yourself—elegiacally, ironically, however you please—or you may eavesdrop on others. These, too, comprise one's company: young men talking of simple suicide, middle-aged men making their necessary compromises difficult, old men ruminating on other lives and different deaths. Though a Men's Room by ancient edict and sign, you will find the occasional woman here. Things are lost and found here: time, a few laughs, and such (for you); the quick passage, beer, and the like (for me). You will be surprised.

One appears here each day to husband his time from noon till six-thirty. People such as yourself come to know one, to sit with him and buy his beer, when they are alone. When one tires, one walks alone along the St. Clair River. Oily rainbows and assorted filth lap its shores in a lovely parody of eternity. One walks no farther north than the Bluewater Bridge, no farther south than the gates to Imperial Oil and the beginning of the Chemical Valley. When one wearies of the night air one returns to the St. Clair Hotel. Within this triangle—bridge, gate, hotel—from whose apex a line can be drawn into the third dimension (one's nondescript room above), one endures indeed. But one waxes self-indulgently.

You come here for rest and relaxation. This is fine and as it should be. Those expectations will also be met. There is no call for concern over being seen to enjoy yourself alone when one is present. For example, you may laugh as freely at your own jokes in one's company as you would snort fearfully at your discontinuous life in lonely circumstances. But you must not expect one to laugh while you are here, as he has heard most jokes before. By way of illustration, the following:

Some time ago an old mailman asked himself at one's table, "Why do dogs lick their own genitals?" He paused too short a time, but let that pass. "Because they can!" he howled freely. After he left, one retired to one's nondescript room above. There, the humorous insight of the joke appeared quite striking: the inexhaustible (it appears) incongruity between aspiration and achievement, the (as it were) bare-balled somatic deflation. (You see already that one is not without a sense of humour. An alternative: First drunk looking at genital-licking dog: "Gee, I wish I could do that." Second drunk: "Don't you think you should pet him first.")

You may choose to bring some of your many superior friends here, to "slum," as they say. One used to caution with vain looks against such indiscretion, but one has come to tolerate, even to see some usefulness in, this perfectly human foible. (The unfaithful spouse is compelled to see the unimaginative mate in the same room with the accommodating lover, and so forth. Why? Because he/she can.) Four warnings, though, in the event of such daring-do:

1. Do not feel anxious.
2. Do not shirk.
3. Do not covertly signal.
4. Do not sheepishly indicate your and your friends' natty attire.

Nor should you secretly send a draft or pitcher to one's table. Nor should you drop a five-dollar bill when you pass on the way to the men's room. Unexpressed affront has been taken at such presumption. One is neither fool nor whore. Though both can be heard and had here. If one is sitting alone when you arrive with your prosperous friends, that is fine. You should consider that one is not here. If another customer is sitting at one's table, that is as it should be. You should use the other's presence to assist the obliteration of one from your considerable conscience. Like the gregarious Bartleby, the scrivener, one prefers it this way.

Should a member of your party look about this dim room and notice one, he will turn to you and say some such thing as, You've been in this hole in the afternoon before, do you know that one over there?

You must feel free to look in one's general direction and say, Who? I see no one. Then slap the table and laugh loudly as you shout your order to the bartender, demanding four of the best goddamned pickled eggs in Beautiful Bluewaterland! Such behaviour will promote camaraderie in your party, may assist a sale or purchase. This is fine and as it should be.

Should a member of your party then order a conciliatory beer sent to one, that too is fine and as it should be. One will lift the gift glass to him only. Thus one makes sympathetic acquaintance.

Should you return alone after your business with your friends is successfully transacted, you must act as though nothing happened between us. Ideally, nothing did. As you order our beer, simply shout at one, What'll yours be? One . . . ? This is fine and as it should be. Your voice argues volumes for your sociability: you could *choose* to be alone. But one does not answer, of course, let alone order preferences. Whatever beer you drink, order two. Similarly, if you must buy our beer in pitchers, order two pitchers. If, after two or three glasses, you feel absolved and eager to be off, do not concern yourself about waste. Simply joke about the shame of leaving good beer . . . what with all the thirsty children in the third world! Laugh, burp loudly if you wish, and leave. One will drink what is left in your pitcher after you have gone.

But if you should choose instead to loosen your tie and drink pitcher after pitcher, or fifteen bottles, or thirty glasses of draft, that is of course fine and as it should be. The beer here is inexpensive, promptly served, and well chilled. You must feel free to get as drunk as you feel inclined. One will stay with you. Nobody has ever been taken from one's table and ejected for simple drunkenness. Allow one to illustrate:

Once upon a time at one's table, a male nurse on the day of his forced retirement threw up beer and partially intact pepperoni sticks. He felt that he had wasted his life in a traditionally female occupation and that "they" should not have been allowed to "boot him out on his fanny anyway." Pathetic? Tut, tut. He was allowed to persevere in a raw drunk, and he proceeded to bounce some memorable times off one.

Another time, a middle-aged gentleman whose assets had been put in receivership silently left one's table. In the men's room he slashed his wrists with a broken bottle. He was back the following afternoon with a detective, a psychiatrist, and an officer of the Salvation Army. The detective demanded to know with whom the gentleman had been sitting the previous afternoon. The bartender answered, "With no one." To the dismay of the Army officer, the bartender then agreed with the psychiatrist that brighter colours might help; however, he insisted that his clientele prefer it here as it is, though he did not look to one for confirmation. The Salvation Army officer was allowed to tape up a poster in the men's room. The poster, barely a pencil sketch, depicted a huge and transparent Jesus Christ standing back of a bank of telephones that were manned by Army personnel. Christ had taken upon Himself the sins of the world, so naturally He wore a look that guaranteed eternal life. And He has been with us for some time now. For purely business reasons— for the sake of one's company—one removed the poster to his room above.

The glasses here are filmed. You are well advised to drink from the bottle.

(Incidentally, you too may choose to consume pepperoni sticks or pickled eggs. Such nutrients may well be bracing for the time of late beers. But one, in his relentless thirst, does not confuse his stomach with victuals. Mind now: never badger one to accompany you to an eatery.)

If you are a frequent binge (i.e., therapeutic) drinker, you will eventually exhaust even your impressive store of self-starring lore. Lest you feel compelled to invent stories about yourself, and so feel guilty the next day, may one presume here to present a list of subjects and idiomatic segues for the time of middle-to-late beers? One directs you to the third column, though you might find some of the first two engaging. In fact, feel free to browse, to read up-and-down, across, or both, or not at all. Here, take it, you commit to nothing.

Lower	Middle	Upper
Unions once filled a need, but now they don't.	Creative financing temporarily saved the housing market/your ass.	Post-modernism, post-structuralism, and the Spasmodics
Dad was a tough old bugger, but principled.	The old man saw it all coming, but would he help?	Androgyny and *fin de siècle* decadence: Jackson, Prince, k.d. lang.
The school of hard knocks	You could have been where *Ms*. M-B-A Armstrong is, but for the kids.	A business degree from Harvard, and they kicked him out on his fanny at sixty-five.
Playboy was better when it stuck to big knockers.	Some of that stuff you can rent is pretty hot, but they keep the hard-core for their own fuck parties on inventory day.	If the big guy can afford to let you go, you may take early retirement to write a novel.
Women don't really want equality.	Statistics show that one of these visible minority woman wearing knee pads can waltz into the exec's can in 2.7 years.	Look at Germaine Greer. Or better not. Haw-haw.

Lower	Middle	Upper
Vasectomies shrivel 'em up like two sunkist raisins and cause lukemia. It's true.	You'd cut it off for a key to the exec's can.	Youth is wasted on women.*
More men have hemmies than will admit it.	Ballbreakers gave you the bleeding ulcer.	The big guy's collection of flagellation imprints is quite striking. But some of that stuff you can rent . . .
You're doin' all right, thank you.	And of course they're off "sick" at least four days every month.*	The young Indian in Purchasing
Let's get serious for a moment.*		See "Middle," item five.
*Order more beer.	*Do a spit take and laugh as though you don't mean it.	*Do not smile or fiddle with your swizzle; one sits still for the aphorism.

The time of late beers will stir up the tender feelings. This confusion of beer and sentiment will prove, one knows, a brewer of bathos. Nevertheless, you must feel free to turn to one of the three walls that protect you here and cry silently and manfully. You will then take a deep breath, knuckle the phantom tear, and talk freely of old loves, of those you hurt with the ambivalence of your passions. One will listen and understand what a lover you were in your day—and are yet, and are yet. Power and passion will salute the unworthy world in the lift of your eyebrows as you toss back your beer. Do not cock even a fleetingly self-conscious eye over the rim of your tilted glass and read passé irony into one's enduring silence. One does not judge. You, on the other hand, must feel free for the sake of flagging monologue to assume that one holds any number of incendiary opinions.

As you consume more and more beer, you will talk of death, naturally, of those who are gone and to whom you never professed your love. Who *is* to say? Yes, it might have helped. . . . *Though*, with regard to the experience of one's life-time, such a profession of love, by having made the deceased happy, would have shortened his/her stay here, and, by alleviating your apparent guilt, your time too. In fact, *had* you professed your love to Dad/Mom/ et cetera, *we would not be here at this time.* Somewhat like one, you will then determine the uselessness of words and conclude with a concession to impenetrable mystery. That is all that can be said, is fine and as it should be. One's silence in this instance should be gainfully employed as mute testimony to your wisdom. Who in his right mind, and after so much beer, could be expected to see, let alone to concede, the uselessness also of . . . "impenetrable mystery", was it? Yes.

Fortified so, you will then revile life, rant, condemn, rave, curse, resolve to rutting indiscriminately. Now we are living! No, indeed not: a growing family and an unbearable mortgage do not constitute psychic emasculation or the death of your . . . dream.

In the morning, when your throat is raw from singing and smoking and snoring and . . . ? No, no. No need to scurry blindly like some cockroach in a suddenly lighted toilet. Forget those wet images that sway like a bale of waterlogged tobacco in your belly. You must feel free to return here, to sit with one and proclaim you are on the waggon. One has been known to forget himself more thoroughly and toast such resolve. What good shepherd having found one lost sheep, et cetera. Or, for that matter, what wolf. Ha, ha. Yes, a joke.

You may of course inquire if you did anything foolish in the time of ultimate beers. If the query alleviates rather than exacerbates anxiety, you must ask. You will selectively recite what you choose to recall of the previous afternoon and end by exclaiming, Jesus H! Imagine! Singing those old Beatle songs! Good ol' Lennon, the big lug. . . . Uh, I didn't . . . ?

Tut, tut. That is all you need bother to remember. All is all right. We were both to drunk to remember. A drunk's memory plays drunken tricks. Sit still for Christ's sake! . . . Pardon, please. One sometimes over-dramatizes. This is fine and as it should be.

Between such low and high spirits—in mid-cycle—you will have time only for a quick beer. In this event, you should consider loaning one some money, ten dollars, say. You see, one has neither low nor high points. Emotionally, one rests outside vicissitude, and one must have his beer. It is disconcerting to one and all the way one's memory can be jarred by thirst and/or financial stringency. One remembers an ungenerous man, a farmer, who blamed his wife and children for the loss of his farm, a fleeting acquaintance who thought guilt over his friend's death could be assuaged with *alternating* rounds of beer, a stingy stranger whose covert greed caused his daughter's madness, a writer of paperback romances . . . But pardon, please. One again reflects self-indulgently on his a-history.

As you move out of these periodic troughs of restorative mediocrity, the number of beers you allow yourself will increase, dramatically some afternoon. You will then come to perceive yet more clearly the relative inexpense of one's enduring silent presence here, especially so when again you enact exactly the same routine of singing and crying in precisely the same detail. But this too is fine and as it should be. And yes, it must have been the solitary drunk at the far corner table who cried lonesomely. I believe he works at the Fiberglass plant. But one makes no claim to perfect recall, only selective (I refer to the small matter of remuneration).

One does reflect overmuch this afternoon, though. At any rate, already you are reading one's thoughts. Do sit and relax. A short quick cold one? Yes. Here.

In Violet Air

Call it whatever you want, but I call it comic relief. Ask Charismatic Peters about comic relief. Shakespeare does it for God's sake! . . . C'mon, look, it was crowded as the standing-room-only hyppo section of hell in that funeral home. Everybody was hanging onto Baker's old lady and boo-hooin' what a terrific guy Paul had been, how smart he could have been if only he'd used *all those brains*. And I *didn't* say it right to old lady Baker, no matter what McIntyre and those hosebags, Blundy and Lowe, have been saying. All I did was stand within earshot of old lady Baker and say to McIntyre, "Shit, I sure hope this doesn't happen to any of the other Baker kids."

Baker's old lady spun round and slapped me so hard my balls jumped for cover. "Throw him out!" she shrieked at the funeral director. "It's all *his* fault!"

And the sweating goof took me by the collar, trucked me through the coffin showroom, and dumped me out back by his big blue garbage bin. I didn't want to hang around in there anyway. I hate crowds.

You'd think I'd said that I hope the rest of the Bakers *do* die like Paul did. Like what was I *supposed* to say? 'Uh, duh, geez, Mrs. Baker, Paul sure was one good guy. Too bad it couldn't have been McIntyre here, eh?' Yah, but McIntyre wasn't standing right there listening, was he?

Look, Baker O-deed on booze and pills. Okay? Purple City really had nothing to do with it. Right? Right. It's not like it was an act of God, and it wasn't an accident. You hyppos get so jittery when some guy who's been slowly killing himself finally does it. You same hyppos who get even more misty when some old shit like John Lennon buys it—somebody you don't even know for God's sake! Or know only from old records, TV and *People* magazine. Some nag's fart like John Wayne bites the dust and guys' mothers bury their flaring nostrils in the *Weekly World News* to snort out which of his horses was the Duker's favourite cornhole. Forget supper for their surviving kids, toss a tear and whip up that yummy Kraft Dinner. Yah! ... So tell me about it. I'm the hyppo? Unos momentos, signor.

When I told McIntyre in the Bluewater Arcade about Baker dying, he turned—fingers still flickin'—and said, "Shit, what a drag. Wonder who he got to buy the booze." Yah, right. But he wasn't Junior Respect in the funeral home, was he? And Blundy and Lowe, I told them at Mr. Submarine, and Lowe said, "Yeah, well, he was okay, sometimes, I guess. But like we all gotta go. Wanna bite?" But in the funeral home the two of them didn't stand holding each other's hands like their waterworks might wash them down a sewer, did they? I'm disrespectful? Tell me about it.

Or look at it this way. McIntyre's old lady has all these, uh, mementos of Elvis Presley all over the house: pictures stuck on all the walls and little beerbellied statues of the pig in front of the bar mirror; and his sweating face on a sweatshirt she always wears, her tits floppin' so that the original greaseball's zillion chins wiggle death-defiantly. She was disgusting the first time I was over there after it happened. Stinking of booze and cigarettes, she tried to bury me in her sagging tits. "I know just how you feel," she whimpered, her eyelashes half unstuck and batting mini-tears at the velvet picture of el greaso behind the bar. "When the King ... when Elvis ... passed ... "

And old man McIntyre, with his brand-new, pre-torn and hemmed T-shirt and styled punker's haircut, he starts into a story about how his best friend bought it in Vietnam. "Hey, can you

heads dig that they did a lotta acid over there? So maybe ol'
Satch—my best friend from highschool, dig it, and a Black—made
the big trip in style." I'm like, uh, hip, Mr—I mean, *Norm*. Then he
gets sidetracked bragging about how smart he was to scoot across
the border at Port Huron to here, the chickenshit. *Whew!* Some-
thing die and rot in here? *Let me out!*

So let's face up to it and get it out of the way: people don't
give wormshit about anything but themselves. And that's why my
little joke in the funeral home (which, by the way, Baker would've
loved) is a *big* deal. Ooo, now the hyppos feel *involved*. Yah, like
involved after the fact, like people who run up to mangled cars and
gasp, "Can I help?" Can I help myself to a closer look? Ooo, isn't
that horrible. I'll bet he was drunk.... Baker hated everything, all
the hyppo bullshit.

In our second-to-last Man-In-Society class, our topic was
Canada's recent achievements. First of all, Baker wondered out
loud if a gigantic intelligent alien would use Canadarm to crank
himself off on Canada.

Charismatic Peters, too cool of course to be phased by mere
sex, just stared at Baker. "Would you like to tell us something
about the masturbatory art, Mr. Baker? A *master*, I'm sure." You're
a born comic, Charismatic, that's what you are. Quit teaching! Go
to Hollywood!

Baker made a quiet kissing noise and cupped the inside of his
thigh.

Then Baker cut in on Phyllis Sowinski—Syphilis-the-Sow—
who'd been gushing about how sexy and heroic that Ken Taylor
guy is. He said loudly to me, "Who gives a living shit if that brillo-
headed goof smuggled a few Yanks out of I-ran? They all work for
the C.I.A. anyway. Besides, that Ayatollah guy don't bullshit. It's
against his religion."

Charismatic stopped grinning like Liberace struck by light-
ning while taking a good crap, and shouted, "Baker!"

"The guy's no hyppo," Baker said. "He sticks to what he
says." Baker looked worried about how he'd sounded. He shot me

a glance and returned to normal: "Even if he does wipe his Ayatollah's asshole with a bone."

"Baker, I read *Playboy*, too. You and it are casting aspersions on a traditional Muslim, uh, ablution which you are too ignorant to appreciate."

"Sounds to me like they don't know their assholes from their bones."

Syphilis-the-Sow swivelled back to the front sucking air up her tilted nose like Baker and me were lines she was trying to snort out of our seats. Baker spread his knees, made a loud kissing noise and jabbed his thumb at his crotch. But Sow and Charismatic were already on to Terry Fox.

"All-in-all, it's been a banner year for Canada. And one hears that there are plans afoot—no pun intended—to attempt Mount Ev—" Charismatic stopped himself at the amazing sight of Baker's raised hand. "Yes, Mr. Ba—Paul? Please, feel free to join us." Charismatic must have grown small bone, standing there wiggling his fingers for Baker to *join* them.

Hands cup-and-saucered on his desk, the meekest, most enquiring frown on his face, Baker cocked his head and said, "Gee, Sir, maybe our class could do something for the retar—like for special exceptional kids."

"Paul?" said Charismatic.

"Yeah, like maybe we could get Magoo Rochester to read a braille version of the encyclopedia, or paint a white line the length of the trans-Canada, or something, and collect money and give it to, uh, those less fortunate than we."

Rochester, with glasses that looked like they were cut from bank doors, hated Paul on sight, ever since Paul tricked him into drillpressing his tie. I made a noise like somebody getting the wind knocked out of him, but I kept pretty still.

"Why, Paul, that's simply a *splendid* idea. Would you be willing to act as homeroom liaison with *Mr.* Rochester. I believe he has a shop class right after this period."

"Yeah, sure."

"And Paul, carry out your assignment with *some* sensitivity. Remark on how Bernard's—*Mr.* Rochester's, to you—touch with wood has improved markedly with his failing sight. You might mention Milton, or Bethoven, but only if you can do so naturally."

I got a piss shiver, and Paul and me exchanged side glances.

"Gotcha. But like I think it would be better than Terry Fox."

"Paul?"

"Well, didn't Fox make it only half way, like?"

"Why yes, Paul, that's correct. Are you, perchance, implying something quintessentially Canadian in the Marathon of Hope? I.e., the mis-hammered last spike? Our new Constitution and the faulty fountain pen with which the Queen—"

"Yah, right. But like wouldn't it be more, uh, appropriate, like beause of the way the guy runs, to call it the marathon of *hop?* "

It was like Baker had cut a loud one in church just before the first tinkle of the Offertory bell. Charismatic just bowed his head and pointed sideways at the door: "Ouuu-t." He couldn't speak for a good minute, so strained you could've sliced a dozen washers off his asshole.

So tell me about it. Baker didn't give a shit about anything. Why should I? Especially now. Anyway, we were both gonna quit school soon as we legally could and head out to Vancouver. Next summer in fact.

And now you hyppos gotta make such a big deal, so other hyppos will think what sensitive assholes you are. You same hyppos who called Baker wimp, twit, jerk, spazz, goof, loser, burnout (your favourite), now you treat me like I'm the one person in the world who hated him. *Me,* his best friend for God's sake! His only friend. Like Blundy and Lowe won't let me do anything till I write a letter of apology to old lady Baker—to be put in the school paper! Hey, tell me about it. Like I pray to the Devil that I never get *that* horny.

At school they're trying to make me go for regular meetings with the guidance counsellor, an old shit who came to school one day with a safety pin taped to his ear. Uh, right on. Power fists and all that. At the beginning of the one meeting I did go to, he tried to slap my hand, but I pulled back at the last split-second and watched the goof stumble into a bookshelf that was spilling psycho tests, pamphlets about Catholic, uh, necking, and health centre brochures about safe sex. Then the twit leaned over to light my cigarette and asked if I'd ever felt, "Mm, you know, *attracted* to Paul?" Sure thing, Saint Freudman, like we took turns reaming each other's holy tarholes every night. But would you mind panting in the other direction, douchebag, your breath smells like a tuna on the rag. . . . Yah, but we weren't in his office, were we? He knew I couldn't drop him there. Next time I'm supposed to go back, he thinks I'm gonna go in the gym with him so we can beat the living shit out of each other with bats of foam rubber. Yah, right, what time was that? Gotcha. . . . *The Living Shit*, that's probably what Baker's gigantic intelligent aliens call the human race.

Mr. Psychology made me take a book by some gimp in Toronto. "A close personal friend," he wheezed. "We're very close on matters thanatological." Yah, like I'll bet, and even closer on matters bum-fucking. But get the title of the book: *The Lie of Death*. Sort of grabs you right by the ol' scrotocular formation, eh? I smoked a joint in the garage, went up to my room and just glanced at the book. I remember the first two sentences: "You, like the vast majority of humanity, probably believe that you are, like most of mankind, going to die. It's a lie." The rest of the book's about a bunch of panicking old turds trying to top each other's "OBEs"— their, uh, "out-of-the-body experiences." *Whew!* Let *me* out! Sounds to me like some kinda psycho definition of puking. Out of their fucking minds would be more like it for these people. I mean it, they claim to be able do something that, if it really was true, would be more fun than fucking. But what do *they* claim to do? They fly over trees, "like in a dream like," visit their neighbours, and then wow the scientific world by reporting what the hyppos down the street had for supper: "You had meat loaf, potatoes, and . . . don't tell me . . . a vegetable! . . . Okay, but I could see it was some kind of meat. Your chandelier obscured my vision." The gimp writer from Toronto keeps reminding you that he's got all the experiences in a computer, so you can't argue with him. And there's a picture of him on the back of the book that shows him wearing a white smock and holding a clipboard.

The truly freaked don't bother visiting their neighbours. They "sojourn" on unknown planets, come back and, amazingly, describe them in endless detail, like to prove they've really been there. "For sport, they have a game sort of like our own hockey, only they don't use defencemen and every team but one—because they have an odd number of everything—gets into the playoffs." What is this, *odd number of everything?* Give me a break. That bullshitter's watched too many Leaf-Oiler games from the Leaf's end. At least with the X-ray specs they advertise on the backs of comics—"See the amazing skeletal structure!!!—they have the sense to show some little fox in a transparent dress just beyond the goggle-eyed perv's big bony hand. But those things are a rip-off too.

Anyway, all these into-the-bullshit experiences build up to cases of people who died but didn't really die. No shit. These hyppos really could redefine what the gimp calls "brain death." But unos momentos, signor. I've got the book right here, uh, somewhere. Read and weep.

"I was undergoing my third bladder operation in as many years, and the prognosis was poor. Suddenly I was over the operating table, hovering like, and I didn't know whether to leave or return." Go! you astral asshole. "I have two lovely young children, you see." Yah, right, like while this one's checking out she's worried that her lovely young kids won't have popcorn to go with a special six-hour *Love Boat*. "Then I was in a long dark tunnel that had a light at the end, and I was aware of the presence of my departed aunt Blaisedelle, the one with the gift. Because I was always her favourite, she had come to guide me. I sensed something else that was eerily familiar, like deja vu, or when you pick up the phone just before it rings, or when you and someone you're talking to say the same thing at the same time." The guy who wrote the book put a string of periods here. "I've always suspected that I, too, have a special gift that way." The woman who has everything. "Oh, it was like something I left when I was born, some power that remains just beyond apprehension in this illusory sojourn." It's called your brain, Lazarus. "It was a warm light like a magnet of love, and I felt this awful pull of overwhelming LOVE!!!" Yes-yes, now we're getting somewhere, I've felt that overhauling pull myself since Blundy and Lowe cut me off. "But then Auntie Blais said that I was not yet prepared to pass over, that Harvey could not carry the mortgage alone at sixteen percent, with a balloon payment coming up, *and* raise the kids in what I consider to be the proper fashion. And just like that, my urologist was waking me up." I hope stupid Harv sued for malpractice. "Life now seems more sacred, more mysterious, and less important to me. I've not had trouble with my bladder since." Piss off.

One thing I know for sure: I'll bet you could go through that whole book and there wouldn't be one case of somebody Baker's or my age. There ain't! Of course not! It's only old farts who're scared to death of dying. Look, nobody's gonna be afraid of drowning in the middle of the Sahara, right? Right.

The thing that pisses me off is that everybody thinks I've gotta be sorry and scared too. Well I'm not. Neither was Baker. Anyway, I tried to tell him to take it easy. Okay?

On our last night together—Baker's last night period (boo-hoo, toss me a tear)—he kept sucking back the pure alcohol, not bothering to mix it with the Gatorade. He was eating so many bennies I thought he'd either pass out or puke. There was only one thing that could bring him back. Though I didn't like using it too much, I said we should do some Purple City.

"Yah," he groaned, his eyes swollen and slitted like a bad fighter's. "Purple City! You an' me, buddyman!"

We were the only two people in the whole world who knew what Purple City was. I discovered it, last Christmas Eve during Midnight Mass at Our Lady of Mercy on the corner of London Road and Christina Street. I'd had to leave the crowded church. The sweet stinking perfume from the old ladies and the boozy cigarette breath from the old men had me ready to honk down the back of the pious hyppo begging favours in front of me. I hate crowds, so did Baker, who said he quit going to Mass when he was seven. And there's nothing like Midnight Mass at Christmas to bring out the hyppos, all pissed up and full of goodwill, wondering if they'd spent more than they'd get back. So I went outside for a breath of fresh air—a real act of faith and hope in stinking Sarnia.

For once the whole world felt empty, still and together. It was clean, simple. Like the Yanks and Russians had finally gotten round to dropping some neutron bombs. The sky was clear and packed with stars. Though there were millions of light years between them. It wasn't cold, either. But I began to feel jittery standing at the front of the church and staring up along the beam that lit the cross. Look, I was already worried about Baker. Okay?

He'd begun drinking and drugging alone, heavily and every day. His old man and old lady didn't give a shit then, neither did his older brothers and sisters. Okay, if they did, they didn't do anything about it. And that's all that matters now, not the boo-hooin'. They did nothing but whine stuff like, "Pau-aul, don't be such a burnout." Then they'd laugh at something he'd say and pop themselves a beer, him another. Because with a few brew in him Paul *was* one funny guy. Then with a few more he was a madman. So there was really nothing I could do. He was too smart for me.

"Look around for Christ's sake," he'd once said, pissed off because we'd not been able to score any brew or bennies. "There's nothing left for us. No work, nowhere to go. The old shits'll soon have a war to get rid of us. Don't tell me about buddy-buddies in our own apartment out West. There is no fucking out West! There's zilch left for us! . . . I'm gettin' outta here."

You couldn't argue with the guy. Sober, he was too smart. Half stoned, he was funnier than Richard Pryor and Eddie Murphy put together. Gone, he was dead to the world. I just didn't know what to do! . . . He'd get mad. Or make fun of me. Okay? Give me a break. Believe me, for the first time in my life I was worried sick about somebody else.

I felt jumpy too outside the church because I was waiting for the hyppos inside to start singing again and ruin everything. I actually thought for a split second to pray. Why not? According to Charismatic Peters, Jesus had all the answers. Yah, right: Oh, Jesus, help-me-help-me-help-me! Cross my heart and hope to die I won't be a hyppo any more if You do. . . . Yah, but Jesus didn't buy it for Himself, too, did He? He knew what hyppos He'd have to grow up with. I mean, shit, just look—one of His own guys turned Him in! Another thing, Jesus was a Jew, right? Right. So how come all through history everybody hates Jews? *Eh?* Case closed. Like the whole of western civilization is hyppo. (That last one about Jesus being a Jew isn't mine. It's one Paul pulled on Charismatic. Charismatic got all jumpy and said that Jesus was a Jew in name only. Whatever the fuck that means.)

So for no good reason I turned and stared into the spotlight. It didn't hurt my eyes, so I moved closer, and closer, till I was standing about ten feet in front of it. I stared until I could make out the shape of the big flat bulb like an A-bomb mushroom, then the spidery filament like jittery lightning. Dear God, give me some new way to distract Baker. I'm the only one he'll even consider listening to. If I give up on him, or chicken out, he'll be totally alone.

I was worried, honest to God. But at the same time I couldn't help thinking how good I was for worrying about Baker. Now that's a hyppo for you.

When I turned away from the light I was blind. Oh my God, what've I done! Baker's cost me my sight! . . . Then the world came back. Everything was purple. The Chemical Valley downriver had a beautiful purple halo. A miracle! I felt light as air. *Whoa*, up on tiptoe. I didn't know what it was, but maybe if I told Baker—

"No-o-el, no-o-el, no-o-el, NO-O-EL! . . ." The hymn brought me right down. Sounded like they were begging God for a break: No-o-hell, no-o-hell . . . *Please* God, tell us hyppos it ain't so, and we promise to fill the church again at Easter, just for You.

I went inside and sat through the last half-hour, everything still purple. I even took Communion, though you're not supposed to full of sin. I returned to my seat, closed my eyes and dared God to strike me dead right then and there. When I opened my eyes the purple was gone. Father—"Call me Pat, just Pat, you hosers"—

Padega came round the altar as usual with his fag's hands steepled on his chest and his pink cheeks beaming like he'd just let the burning bush sit on his face.

I shoved my hands in my pockets when Padega told us to turn and wish our neighbours a Merry Christmas. Yah, right, we're groovy Catholics. I stared at the wheezing old shit beside me with a look that said, Touch me, goof, and I'll break your thumbs so you never touch anybody again. When everybody was leaving, I made it a test to twist and slide sideways so I didn't even brush anybody. When Padega stuck out his paw at the door, I gave him a look that said, Back off, bullshit artist. But I wasn't really pissed off. I was as giddy as a kid with a gift: a secret, a riddle, and a mystery for Baker, all in one.

And Purple City became a secret between just Baker and me. For a while it worked. Sometimes to bug the other kids we'd let the name slip. For a while the others had an excuse to talk to Baker, and he tolerated them.

Wendy Shaeffer, of all people—a nun-in-training if ever there was one—came closest to blowing the cover: "*I* know what it is. It's when they drape all the statues and the Eucharist in purple during Lent, like now. Ha-ha, I got it. You think you're *so* smart, Paul Baker. You and your buddy Benning."

"Slut," sneered Baker. "Only thing you've got is shit for brains and a twat like where the gym dividers meet."

In Baker's last Man-In-Society class, Charismatic Peters asked us to name "natural ways of getting high."

Shitface Shaeffer had a list ready: visiting croaking old people who don't even know *they're* in the room, free babysitting for Sarnia's whining welfare cases when they go out for supper, teaching crippled kids to run the high hurdles, and on and on and on.

Baker whispered loudly, "Purple City."

Charismatic came stomping down the aisle to the second-last desk and stared at me in the last: "What, Mr. Benning, *is turtle city?* We've all been excluded quite long enough from your and your *boyfriend's* secret."

Yah, right, we're homos. You gotta wonder why Charismatic always tries to get you with that one, eh? "I didn't say it, sir. Baker did. He's always talking aloud, disrupting the class, and distracting me from your informative and, if I may say so, entertaining lectures." I heard Baker snort a laugh. "And I think, sir, that the troubled youth said *purple* city." I can talk any way I want. So can Baker.

Baker pulled a straight face: "Sir, it's when, sir, you go to church, sir—"

"I told you!" Wendy Shaeffer squealed, then nearly melted at her first searing look from Charismatic. His head vibrates and his eyes bug like he's squeezing out a totem-pole turd.

But what was Baker doing! My eyes burned.

"Baker," barked Charismatic like Mr. Commando in Christ's guerrilla corps, "I won't tolerate blasphemy. And if you go out this time there's no coming back."

"Unos momentos, Mr. signor," said Baker. "Like I mean it. You go into church during Lent, just like Miss Shaeffer said. You face the purple-draped host and do this." Baker stood in the aisle, sort of dipped, grabbed his crotch with both hands, pulled up on it and made a loud kissing noise: *"Tell, me, about, it!"*

Charismatic went stumbling backwards down the aisle like he was falling down a bottomless well: "Out! Out! Out! . . .

That was the closest we ever came to giving Purple City away. Now everybody knows. Baker was a hot item in the *Sarnia Spectator:* "Sarnia Boy Dies of Drug/Light(?) Overdose."

But look, the point of it all is that I could already see that Baker was on his way down and out last Christmas, I tried still, Purple City just wasn't enough, or it was too much. . . . But let's not get all misty and confused. It's really quite plain and simple.

That last night, I had to put one of Baker's arms around my shoulders, mine around his waist, and all but drag him down to Our Lady Of Mercy. Whenever I eased my hold, he slumped to the ground and lay there with a tired sneer on his face. At OLM I stood and balanced him on the front lawn before the big wooden double doors. I was fishing in my pocket for a roach when he threw out his arms and screamed clearly: "Tell me about it!" He fell flat on his face and powdered a few chunks of white dog shit that had made it through the winter.

I turned him over and tried to shake him awake: "Burnout, you really sick?"

He puked pinkish slop out the side of his twisted mouth and sort of wagged his tongue at it. He reminded me of that hose in *The Exorcist*. I had to laugh. What else could I do?

I sat him up, grabbed his collar and dragged him over to the spotlight. He collapsed against the big aluminum socket, then kind of hugged it. Holding on, he made it to his knees and hauled himself around to face the light.

"Not so fucking close!"

But he moved his head even closer. "Tell ... me ... about. . . it," he whimpered and touched his eyeballs to the glass.

I jerked him away. Maybe I shouldn't have waited so long. Okay?

He flopped onto his back, arms spread, eyes wide open. He sort of laughed and cried silently at the same time. "I can't see a thing," he said, sounding stone-cold sober all of a sudden. Then he sighed, "My purple universe," closed his eyes and began jerking about on his stomach like he was trying to fuck the ground.

His purple universe? The ungrateful burnout. I stepped forward and stared into the spotlight. I was nearer than I'd ever been before because I figured I had some catching up to do. I could feel the heat, my eyeballs hurt. That close the filament looked like jittery forked lightning. I got lost thinking. Was the burnout worth all this trouble? If I took him to Van I'd have to look out for him all the time. I'd be the only one who worked, caring for him like he was a brain-damaged brother. ... Still, he was the smartest guy I'd ever known. Really. And Baker knew he was a genius. Ask the guidance counsellor. Baker said he'd been told that he had the highest IQ in the history of the school. That's why Charismatic

Peters hated Baker, because Baker knew everything was bullshit and didn't want to be anything. Just like me.

When I turned away I couldn't see a thing, just a flesh-coloured blankness, a peachy brightness, and I could hardly breathe. It was like I was crowding *myself*, my own body! And it took longer than ever for the world to return. Then I had barrel vision worse than ever. And things weren't purple, they were . . . I don't know, white almost, then white around a point of black, like burning charcoal ready for the meat. I could hear my brain sizzlin', actually imagined I could smell it frying, a stink like sulphur in the lab. Baker wasn't where my barrel vision pointed. And here it comes hyppos, snuggle up and get smug: I was glad. Period. I hadn't even wanted to go *this* far, and now look where he'd led me.

I slowly cranked my head about like a gun on a tank, and spotted Baker stumbling near the evergreen bushes at the side of the church steps. It was like looking down a tunnel that had a. . . Hey, wait a minute. Just like Mrs. O.B.E., eh? Fuck off. Baker stood bent backwards, arms held like he was going to hug the church, head tilted to the steepled cross and the crowded sky. He was mumbling something I couldn't make out for fear my vision wouldn't widen this time. Then it did. The normal purple came oozing in from everywhere like oily waves. Relieved I had to snort a last laugh at Baker's final few staggering steps in my old Purple Universe.

He walked stifflegged into an evergreen bush like a Christmas drunk into the living room looking for a kiss and a good hug from your fourteen-year-old sister, draped himself across it, then rolled off to the side and lay perfectly still. I carried him into the church and dumped him in the little on-deck pew for the Confessional. I got Padega at the rectory and he phoned for the ambulance. It turned out Baker wasn't only dead but stone blind. I'll admit the blind part worried me too for a while, at first more than Baker's being dead. For obvious reasons.

After I got thrown out of the funeral home, I went to the Bluewater Arcade and met this goof who'd just come back from out West. He looked like he was at least thirty: long greasy hair like on a die-hard metal groupie who thinks some fat made-up rocker on Power Hour is the Devil, sleazy eyes, and a needle freak's yellow-green skin. But when he flipped out his wallet to prove how much money he'd made, I checked out his driver's licence and saw that he was only eighteen—just a couple of years older then me. Anyway, he decided me. Imagine all that bread for screwing rich old hosebags! That's right, the guy said I could be a hooker out there. Give me a break. Let's get this show on the road. And I'm pretty good at it. Just ask those scuzz, Blundy and Lowe, if they remember the good old days.

The only thing I regret about being thrown out of the collective boo-hoo at the funeral home is that I wanted to be there to see Baker buried. And I'd have stayed to see them fill in the grave, not like you hyppos, all holding hands and making a community hot tub of the grave with your purple waterworks.

So you can either put all this in your paper as my apology to old lady Baker, or you can clip it into joined dolls and cram it up your collective asshole. But don't waste your time trying to get ahold of me. I'm heading out to Van today, where nobody can touch me.

Assault Nets Fine

Patrick sat in the kitchen leaning over the scarred surface of the big brown table and staring at the ragged nails of his knitted fingers as he'd once stared at the unmendable blades of a plow that had struck an immovable rock. From above came the intentional pounding of feet; the overhead bulb quivered, casting jigging shadows on the old man's nails so that his fingertips appeared to be vibrating. Without turning or changing his expression he tightened his grip and whispered, "Go on. You too. All of you."

Pat eyed his father sideways but didn't lower his head. The frayed cord dangling the bare bulb was fixed ridiculously to the ceiling by a spider web. His mother screamed whenever she saw a spider. He stepped to the counter and picked up his cap.

"I'll slop the hogs then."

"Hogs your arse. Aren't they taking them, too, tomorrow."

"Not their fault, can't let 'em starve." That was not like the old man, who cared more for the stock than for his family. Pat eased the screen shut behind and breathed deeply.

Michael thumped down the steep stairs to the kitchen, the new suitcase banging against his knee. He hurried to the screen door, halted with his hand on its frame and shouted into the evening: "You're crazy!" He half turned: "Mom's right, you really do need a psychiatrist."

"Go on. Out with yeh. No better than the rest."

Afraid that he would cry, Michael faced the screen and inched it open: "Yeah, right. We're all wrong. You're the only one who's ever right. Did you ever consider the feelings—"

"Out."

Patrick stood at the sink window and watched Michael hurry stiffly to the barn. He reached for the sill that needed paint badly, hesitated, then reached to the overhead shelf and took down the old photo album. Without so much as glancing out the window again he returned to the kitchen table. He brushed the mess of bills and bank statements to one side, slipped his hands under the opened album, gripped its top and jammed its base against his breast bone. His head circled slowly, his gaze trailing from photo to photo. They'd not been able to afford the luxury of many. On the first page James, his oldest, passed from diapers to coveralls. In the top left corner his wife, in her new yellow sundress, lifted James to him seated on the new tractor; in the bottom right James drove the tractor for the first time. The second page was Collin, the third Robert, followed by Terrence, Thomas, Michael, and Pat last, named for himself finally, the seventh son of a seventh son. Wasn't that supposed to be lucky? . . . Aa, but he'd leave too. He flipped back the pages and stared at the first photo. Peg, always wantin' a new dress. The ungrateful hooer.

Pat's hand paused in the cloying slop when he heard the barn door, but he kept his head down and continued mixing. "The runt's died. You'd better get it out."

"What'er you stayin' for? C'mon, he's cracked."

Pat slowly clenched his fist and watched the mealy slop extrude. Ignoring his brother, he hoisted the pail and headed for the back of the barn. Slop the hogs, if you can call one old sow the hogs. He was passing the empty cattle stalls when Michael grabbed his shoulder and half turned him.

"Wait a minute. Where are you gonna go tomorrow? Mom wants us both with her. She said forget what she said about finishing school here."

He twisted away and proceeded to the pigpen. He emptied the slop into the trough and waited. The sow stopped snuffling the runt and lumbered over. While she fed, the piglets squealed below her chafed teats. He stepped over the rail and went to the runt, picked it up by the hind legs and dropped it into the bucket. He moved towards the back door.

"You thought I was him!" Michael shouted. Didn't you? You'll never give up. Or grow up. ... Okay, stay with him. You'll be sorry. See if I care."

He stood stock still as soon as the door slammed shut behind him. He had heard the beginnings of crying in Michael's whining. *That's* what had made him unable to answer. But then Michael, his mother's pet, had always been more the baby than he ever was. How could they do it! Abandon the old man? There was no point now in blaming him. Sure he should have sold out last year, but the banks were as much to blame for that. Telling him what to feed, what to plant, how to farm. Besides, the rates could have come down sooner. Then they'd all be saying he was a genius. He should have done this, he should have done that. Who could know his mind?

He puffed his cheeks, then slowly emptied his lungs and looked up at the darkened sky. Unfathomable depth, inconceivable distance, uncountable stars clear like they never were in town, like they never could be in the city. His last night, he felt the barn massive at his back. He remembered its construction, carrying beer to the men, the outdoor feasts served by his mother, the reined joy, and the old man half-drunk taking him up on the roof to drive the last nail while his mother stood below, her apron to her mouth. He breathed deeply. He needed a sack, a good stone. Dump the runt in the pond. That would be an end of it.

Patrick had the pickup loaded before Pat was up. He had sat up till three, then worked till six. He had left the heavy kitchen table where it was because the new rooms, what they were, were furnished. At the foot of the stairs he hesitated. They could all go to the devil and take the whole kip with them! He should leave quietly by himself, and keep going. Leave what cash he had, the

key to the new rooms. The boy would be better of with his mother
and the whole ungrateful pack of them. Not that he wanted their
thanks. ... He looked into the small ornately framed mirror by the
foot of the stairs, and he was looking into the old well that he had
replaced only after a fight; he squinted hard, but the mirror was
still the old well falling away from a small enough mouth to
darkness and silence forever. He shouldn't mind that so very
much. . . . He gripped the banister and shouted, "Get going!"

He sat in the cab and stared straight ahead when he heard the
screen door. In the side mirror he saw Pat, bare from the waist up,
standing on the stoop in those baggy grey sweating pants he wore
to bed.

Pat rubbed his eyes with his fists, stretched and yawned. "I
want some tea first. Do you?"

As though this were a morning for work just like any other.
But he remembered the kettle and the two mugs he'd thought to
leave on the table. He breathed deeply and felt the old tingling
down the length of his gullet. He looked in the side mirror and
noticed again the few long ridiculous hairs that had appeared
around his son's nipples. *His* eyes were as sharp as ever. He let
himself grin quickly before Pat finished his second stretch. They
would plant in twenty days or so.

"You didn't pack the kettle, did you?"

"No, I didn't. Get moving or I'll leave you here to rot." Tall,
he'd reached his full height, the youngest and the tallest. Too thin
though. The milk and sugar! The boys took milk and sugar! He
slapped the steering wheel.

"What's your hurry? You want tea or not?"

"Hmph." And the shadow of hair where the loose pants
hung from the crack of his arse. The two of them could make—
could have made the place pay yet. The boy was old enough
to . . . How old was he?

The tea made, Pat didn't know what to do with the old man's.
Carry it out to him? His mother had always done that, setting the
mug beside him without a word. Call him in? But how? They
never addressed one another. Father? Dad? Daddy? Or simply

shout, It's done. The screen slapped and he started again. The old man was so impatient to be off. To what?

He carried the two mugs to the table. He had set them down before noticing that the chairs were gone. His throat tightened. He picked up his mug and sipped the scalding tea. Strong and bitter, but better then he'd expected without milk and sugar. His father took the other mug and headed for the door.

"What about the table?"

"We've no use for it where we're goin'."

He traced only his own initials, which he'd cut into the big square table before his seat with the jackknife he'd gotten for his twelfth birthday. As he'd expected the old man had strapped him for that. It was the one time any of them were strapped. The old man could never help but snort a little as he hung the razor strop behind the door of the cold storage. His mother had sighed, "Well that, please God, is an end of it." And the old man had grinned so at the fresh scars in the worn-smooth table that she had hurried to the washtub with a mountain of laundered clothes.

The engine roared, coughed and died, whined, caught and was gunned. He couldn't just leave him.

For three weeks Patrick had studied the pitches until early morning in the small kitchen of the three-room apartment above the hardware store. At sixty-six, he was by far the oldest trainee in the course, so he had to study hard. The others, teachers mostly, looked in their forties, though he was finding it difficult these days to tell ages. And the Amway recruiter had tried his damnedest at the interview to dissuade him, relenting only when convinced that Patrick had lived in the area since coming from the old country and knew all the farms for twenty miles around.

He needn't have begged at all, but he had to have the promised money. And not as . . . supplemental income. Teachers were paid too much as it was, with their swanky suits and dandy manners. Only a farmer could sell another farmer. "You'll be in the *sales* field now," the recruiter had grinned by way of relenting. He'd be a farmer yet! Though it would be hard to get money out of farmers. A silk purse of a sow's ear, as Peg had always said of him.   Blood from stone, as he'd often told that hooering loan manager at McCarthy's. Gouging bastard and his bank like an unblighted Babel! . . . A hard sell indeed. So he'd studied until the print blurred and his head near split. If the recruiter hadn't lied too much, he'd have enough in three years to pay down on the Connor place. And Pat at fifteen was as good on a farm as—better than any man!

When Pat came home from school during the first week, his father would cluck his tongue and toss what he'd been reading onto the pile covering the card table that served for a kitchen table. But he always forgot to close the notebook, the pages of which, lined by his surprisingly neat printing, were proof of his deadly earnestness. At night the light from the kitchen kept Pat awake, where he lay on one of the two cots that occupied the main room. The second week, his father no longer feigned casual study bordering on contempt, and only set aside his texts for the meals Pat prepared. In the third week he ate while he studied.

  Every morning he shaved, put on his cleanest shirt and the tie that choked him.   Or it could have been the unfamiliar daily scraping of the blade that intensified the ruddiness of his cheeks. Though that still didn't explain his eyes. They were shining black, skittish, and ringed by warty flesh. Bags like spent udders made him look suddenly like an old woman. He needed rest, not the unnatural reading. The sight of him hunched over his lessons made Pat think of some giant struggling with a broken wristwatch. And that pathetic picture made the teasing at school bearable, though only when Pat was home. Home?

  Home. His mother and brothers had rented an apartment in Sarnia sixteen miles away, though they called it a *townhouse.* James and Collin had found work at a garage that installed only mufflers. Robert, Terrence and Thomas had gotten part-time jobs as waiters in a place that served only hamburgers as big as cowpies, hamburgers that didn't even taste like meat. "They fill them with soy bean!" Michael had laughed the first time he showed up at the school with his mother to convince Pat to come away. "And the people don't even know it!" They were all making good hard cash now, Michael had said seriously the third time they showed up. He had enrolled in the big Catholic highschool. And though he'd been put back a grade and made to take a four-year technical programme, for his own good, he was sure that Pat's grades would let him stay where he was.

"Guess what my school's called," challenged Michael.

He said nothing.

"St. Patrick's! Can you believe it!"

His mother smiled apprehensively, teasingly: "And our new parish has special scholarships to the university for . . . What was it the priest called him, Micky?"

"Promising rural students."

"This *promising* rural student is already staying *where he was*." He turned to leave, then turned back: "I don't want you coming here again." He was talking too much.

She started crying: "Pat, you can't stay with *him*."

Slight as she was, in a pinch she'd been able to pitch bales with the best of them. Now she looked old and frail, if made up more stylishly than before. Her whimpering made it less difficult not to betray what he was feeling.

"Be reasonable," Michael said, his palm held out, showing off the new faceless watch worn on the wrong side of his wrist.

"No more." It was easy.

"What's *he* ever done for you?" she whimpered. "Tell me that? He could have sold out a year ago and taken the job working the Connor place if he cared for any of us. We'd all be well off today. But not him. Selfish and pigheaded till we're put out on the road. Pat, now I'm telling you this for your own good, so help me God I am. But he's never concerned himself over any one of you. You know I'm right. You don't owe him nothing."

She met his eyes and closed hers: "Look at you, Pat, already you've grown more like him."

"Look at me? Listen to yourself."

"Child, we have to bring him to his senses. Someone has to—"

"By leaving him. Do you think *he'd* come crawling after?"

She tugged the new yellow sweater closer to her throat and reached her right hand. He stepped back. "Tell me," she cried openly, "What's *he* ever done for *you?*"

"That's not the point."

"We'll come again—"

"No more." That made them step back. Nothing to it.

"Pat, he needs help, he needs . . ." She ended in sobs and leaned against Michael, who turned and supported her to the car as though from the scar of a fresh grave. In a movie. Yes, a woman in a horror movie.

So he checked the impulse to run after them with a hatred that, for all its imposed objectivity, frightened him still—his body lunged but his feet were rooted. He turned and walked rigidly home. *Home,* he would take the job in the hardware store. *Home,* school was for kids. *Home.*

He'd beaten them all! The teacher told the class that Patrick's grades were the highest anyone had ever received, including himself, he'd joked, making mock of Patrick's achievement. Back in his rooms, he thought of going downstairs to the store and having Pat fetch him a frame for the certificate. He thought better of it, went and sat on the toilet. When he finished his business, he wiped himself with the useless paper. He stood and stared down at the mess. Now that was a childish thing to do. But thank God for small favours; he'd been constipated for weeks.

Aa, money's the genuine article, selling's the true test. That's what the teacher had said. And, to give the Devil his due, he was right for once. He'd show them the damnedest sight of selling since Christ kicked them pack of Jews from the temple! First he'd have to get himself a used station waggon, on time of course, trade in the old truck. But if that hooer's get wasn't lying, he'd have it paid off in not time. Then the boy—then Pat could go back to school, if he wanted. Though he couldn't see why a big strapping fellow like Pat needed any more schooling. Money's the ticket nowadays.

He slipped into his suspenders, snapped them, reached down and cradled his crotch. He remembered, jammed the heels of both palms to his temples, then tugged up the waistband with thumbs and forefingers as the teachers did. He walked evenly to the card table and swiped all the books and pamphlets onto the floor. He picked up the new suitcase, went back to his cot and set the case on it. He deftly sprung the clasps and flipped up the lid. "Here," he smiled with a sweeping gesture at the contents, "we have everything of a sanitary nature for the . . . the . . . the contemporary household! For shiteing Jesus' sake!" The opening pitch of the exam's oral portion had earned him his lowest mark.

But it was all goddamned foolishness anyway. He would simply say hello, talk of the weather, prices. That's the way to sell farmers, what that connivin' imp condemned as the soft sell. "For instance, this handy item, Bactoguard, is Amway's most popular disinfectant." And he whispered, "Spray it up your arsehole." He reached for the container and caught a ragged thumbnail on the suitcase lining. "Shite!" . . . But yes, during the private send-off pep talk the teacher *had* mentioned his nails. And his suspenders, and his boots, and his cap. "It's a nice cap, Pat, but just not in keeping with the image that Amway wishes to project. If you insist upon headwear—and I'll frankly admit, it does take off a few years—perhaps a featherless alpine would better complement that suit. Need I remind you again? It is the farm*wives* with whom you will be transacting *business*." The sassy devil. "I'll knock that grin to the other side of your head for yeh!" Had he talked out loud again?

He glanced over his shoulder at the other cot. He swiped the cap off his head, slipped a nail under the sweatband and tore both band and thumbnail. He composed himself. "Here . . . we have every contemporary nature for the san—Goddamn yeh anyway for a cunting hooer!" He snatched the cap from the cot, failed to keep it crushed, so flung it by the brim at the one filthy window, and missed. Blood dripped from his thumb into the suitcase. He grabbed the Bactoguard, held it at shoulder level, jammed down the button and sprayed himself in the eyes. Eyes burning and

blinded, he stumbled into the bathroom; groping along the wall of
the unfamiliar room, he missed the sink and banged his shin
against the toilet bowl. He knelt, lowered his head inside the bowl
and scooped the unflushed water into his eyes.

He cursed the toilet while he washed at the sink. He snorted
at his bumbling, brought himself to look in the mirror and chuck-
led. Peg, and now Pat too, was always at him about flushing. He
burst into silent, convulsive laughter and crumbled to a sitting
position on the floor. When he recovered, the sweat chilled him.
With his bleeding thumb in his mouth he felt lonelier than he'd
ever felt, and frightened. And ashamed. It was like the mornings
after his few amnesic drunks at The Swill. He tried but couldn't
remember the farm. What had he done in the last few minutes?
And before that? For a long moment a cold black silence snuffled
about him, he cowered and shivered against the wall beneath the
sink, and for a time they occupied the same space, that snuffling
emptiness and he, and he felt nothing.

What if she had a point? What if the old man did need help, a
headshrinker? He'd sure been acting weird since he started selling
that soap for *Scam*way. Ate little when he took the time, so drove
about in that gas-guzzling waggon from six till six on an empty
stomach, then spent his evenings mapping the next day's route.
Doesn't talk at all, answers in grunts. Mumbles to himself con-
stantly, snatches of weather reports, catch-lines like prayers from
his sales pitch, patches of conversation from the past, as though *she*
was here. And his fits of raving about buying the old Connor
place—another farm at his age! And old lady Connor doesn't even
own the Connor place any more. But what's worst is his banking
on getting them back. That's what he's saving for. No money from
him, all of it stashed in that old album, which he handles like it was
some newborn chick. If it wasn't for the scab's wages the hardware
pays, there'd be no food on the table and no roof over our heads.

Pat stood fingering the coarse grey blanket on the unmade
cot, determined this time to leave the crumpled mess as it was. If
it was to work, the old man *had* to learn to do his share. At least he'd

gotten better about flushing the can lately. Tucking the sheet under the mattress, Patrick stubbed his fingers against the album. He slipped it out and immediately dropped it onto the cot. He'd thought the old man always kept it, his farmer's bank, with him.

He went to the window, cleaned a spot with his forearm and looked down at the deserted intersection. A light rain had been falling since dawn. Joe Thompson stepped out of McCarthy's Bank, rubbed his hand across his balding head, and walked off forgetting to put on his cap. He stepped into a flooded hole and pitched forward as though he'd received a blow on the back of his head. He shook his foot, turned his big face to the sour sky and laughed madly. He seemed to consider briefly, then headed back to The Swill, which was kitty-corner to the bank.

I should get outta here. Not that I need his thanks for staying, or his money. But because he doesn't even seem to know I'm here. How'd I get into this mess! . . . He'd starve of course, they'd put him out on the street. Her shrieking complaint as the stock and machinery were being carted off: "They'll put us out on the road!" She's put him out of his head. All of them, running out like rats from a burning barn. More to blame than the banks. He fed me, put a roof over my head. He gave me that. And who knows what he felt, what he's feeling. You could never go by how he acts or the little he says. Nothing real shows anyway. When he strapped me I didn't show anything, and I didn't even feel a thing until later in the loft, and then only warmth, leaning against the old mower in the dusty beams of sunlight, and then a . . . a tickle all through me, like someone was drawing that beam of dusty sunlight and the whole farm through me from head to toe, and I loved everyone, everything, even him, and the farm was mine. This work and worry won't kill *him*. He's used to worse. It's the getting money that's gone to his head. No wonder. At least his fine feathered hat will keep it dry.

He pressed against the window, looked round the three opposite corners of the intersection and at the grey stubbly fields beyond. He drew back his fist but landed it softly on the window pane. He moved stealthily to his father's cot and opened the

album. Taped to the inside of the cover he found seventy dollars
and change. He pinched the neatly ruled page on the facing
photographs, careful not to let it touch his damp palms. In the
neatest print were the names of every family for thirty miles
around, half of whom Pat had never heard. The dates in the
margin showed that his father visited a minimum of twelve farms
a day, each day ending with a call on old lady Connor. The name
of each family was followed by a dash and the notation "ns." After
each Connor a small sum had been entered: $9.89, $8.66, $6.06,
$3.33, $1.01.

No sale. And his one paying customer old lady Connor, dirt
poor and an invalid to boot. They'd been their only close friends,
the Connors. But after old man Connor died, she'd pretty well shut
herself off and leased her fields to some agribusiness. And boy did
the old man hate that word. "Agribusiness my agri-arsehole!
Aggravation's the word!" It was the banks behind the whole
business, so far as he could see. Three months tramping about the
county and this is all he has to show for it. Just better than a buck
for each year of his life.

He replaced the album. With his fingers knitted behind his
head, he lay on his father's half-made cot. Rain pattered the
window more insistently. Fine cracks radiated from the sagging
centre of the damp-spotted ceiling like webbing about to drop. His
mother hated spiders, screamed when she saw one. The old man
was the one cracking. Michael was right. The old man was caught,
had trapped himself really, and he'd have to gnaw off his head to
get free. He should get out while the gettin' was good.

But he never would get out. His allegiance was as inexpli-
cable as his father's stubbornness. Explaining to himself, he
allowed those memories that were as clear as after an early
morning rain to rush in and buoy his resolve. He remembered
James being strapped, the twelve-candled cake after supper that
day, and on everyone's day; the way the old man had smiled to
himself when he passed through the kitchen that time, because
Collin lay across his half-carved initials pretending to have the
bellyache; building the barn; the new tractor; the reined pride in

them all when poor relatives visited. . . . But when the memories ebbed murkily, nothing was explained.

Good things happen, then bad things happen, the old man gets credit, the old man gets blamed. We control nothing of any importance. Good things, bad things, credit, blame—all explanations are just a sick joke we play on ourselves. Because there's nothing even to play it on us. When things are going well the explanations sound great. But even the banks, the big money men, are just running wildly like chickens looking for their heads. And there are no heads. Where we thought the head was there's nothing, cold black nothing. We have nothing, nothing but each other's warm bodies. So they left him out in the cold with nothing, nothing but me.

"Ahoy there!" he called, saluting in the one way he could stomach of the twenty his teacher had recommended. "Amway man requesting permission to come aboard!"

"Come in out of the wet, Paddy," the shrill voice answered. "And for the love of all that's sacred, stop talking like such a blathering fool."

He stamped his new, scuffed, porous brogues and shook himself. Like some old bitch gone in the tooth, perished with the cold and damp. It was all a body was worth to get in a door finally. He looked at himself in the facing mirror. Instead of the gaunt old man in the limp-feathered alpine hat, he saw himself as he had been thirty years before, weathered and hale, come into his own home after a day in his own fields.

He would make her take down that mirror. There was no call always to be gawkin' at yourself. He'd knock down the whole wall, make her fancy sitting room part of a bigger kitchen. Wasn't she wantin' a big new expensive table? They'd be needing the room, his crowd was growing. And there was nothing to stop him having more . . . though she'd had trouble with the last one, little Pat. Or so she claimed. Always something to complain about. If it's not pining after indoor plumbing, it's wanting a television, or

swanky pants for them that's at school. . . . Aa, be fair now, she'd
bourne it, and given him all sons. Ha! He'd get more out of her yet!

He wiped his hands along the narrow lapels of his checkered
suit. Soaked to the bone, and them that once knew him without the
common decency to offer a cup of tea. But he'd not bothered too
many men today. No sirree! . . . But the dry warmth of the barns,
the smell of stock, proved too inviting. A wet day, a day for
tinkering with the machines. Without looking up, the men had
told him to see the wife. Still, a couple had used his first name.
That was something. . . . It was more than flesh could bear.
Mortified, he'd gone back to his waggon and not bothered the
wives.

No, no call for that, he said to himself in the mirror, straight-
ening and tightening the knot of his tie. And he'd not even
intended to sell the men, just talk, arse about for a spell. . . . Now
that godawful mirror's coming down. No two ways about it. Sell
it! Sell everything!

He winked at himself. I've this old hooer right where I want
her. "Are you in bed then?" he called, hating the sound of his voice.

"In here, Paddy."

Aye, she would be. Me famished, and not a bite on the table,
I'll wager. Another of her dandy headaches. And them all away
at school but young Pat. She's the one. Keeps them there and three
of them fit to be a help to me here now. A spiteful devil, hates it here
and always has. Turning them against me. Out gallivanting over
half the county like a born fool and not two pennies to rub together.
Aa, but maybe it is for the best they're away, so's they won't end
up like their old man. She'll make them all bankers! But young Pat.
Isn't he the one! He'll stick by me. We'll have this old place in fine
shape in a couple of months. Then we'll all be together again.

He took the neat white handkerchief from the top pocket and
mopped his brow. Failing to fold the handkerchief into a triangle,
he threw it at the mirror. I won't go grovelin' like some old bitch
that's been kicked too many times! And there the hanky lay, polka-
dotted, snot-caked. He crammed it into his back pocket.

He paused in the doorway to the bedroom and, as his eyes adjusted to the darkness, slowly filled his lungs with the room's dank odour

She lay propped by a pile of crushed pillows, wearing a man's burgundy cardigan buttoned to her chin. She patted the bed: "Come rest over here, Paddy, and tell me all about your day. But first let's us put the kettle on." Exhausted, she closed her eyes and drew a long hoarse breath.

He took her upper arm and helped her from the bed. Below the cardigan she wore a ratty pair of men's long underwear cut off above the knees. She leaned against the stove while he filled the kettle and set it on the heating element.

"I've some soda crackers, Paddy. I know I have," she whimpered. "And I think there's still a spot of blackberry jam. . . some . . . where."

He supported her back to the bed, where she lay on top of the covers. He sat on the edge. He turned to her, touched her knee, her stomach under the cardigan, cupped her cheek, leaned forward and kissed her full on the mouth. She continued smiling, as though nothing had happened.

He flipped up the lid of his case, made his sweeping gesture, and began: "Here, we have everything of a sanitary nature for the contemporary home—"

"Pa-trick," she whined petulantly, "the album. *I want to see the children first today.*" She crossed her arms: "Or I'm buying nothing."

He spoke firmly: "Mary, there are no children today. I left them at home with young Pat. Now you be a good girl and pay attention."

She cried, "I want to see the children first this time. You do your business figures and let me look at the snaps."

Clucking his tongue and shaking his head he shut the case and reopened it: "Here, we have everything . . ."

She could afford nothing that day. No matter, her place was as good as his. It was all clear now, a clear title. He saw himself and her as though he were looking down from the ceiling of that death-smelling room, and then as if the two of them were figures at the illuminated bottom of a dry well he'd been peering into for the longest time. He saw it all—the whole of his life—with frightening and fascinating objectivity.

The preliminary report in the city newspaper brought the estranged family to the pre-trial hearing. At a signal from (Mrs.) Margaret O'Connel, the faimly of six boys stood together and left the courtroom early when Patrick O'Connel's guilt proved incontestable. The summary report of the trial was headlined, "Assault On Semi-Invalid Nets Fine."

Only Patrick O'Connel, Jr., remained throughout the trial. Sitting behind his father he occasionally refilled O'Connel's glass. Other than that, he sat still and expressionless, as did the father.

The defence lawyer argued that O'Connel had suffered enough. He described the incident as "peculiar, bizarre, out of the ordinary, inexplicable." He noted that the agent who leased the woman's land had found her in what was for her a "normal condition" the next day. He emphasized that even the agent had not reported his suspicions regarding the incident to the Regional Police for several days. "The woman was not harmed in any way," he concluded. "The incident, which was not of a sexual nature, lasted only a few seconds. She was kissed. That was all."

The crown attorney pressed for a reformatory term. He pointed out that the victim was "easy prey," and that O'Connel had exploited his position of trust to violate the privacy of a feeble-minded semi-invalid who lived alone in a rural area.

O'Connel chose not to testify in his own defence.

In his decision the judge said he was convinced of O'Connel's guilt, though he believed that O'Connel "was not planning anything improper when he approached the woman's home." He noted that O'Connel had led a good life as a farmer in the area, had raised a family, and had no "selfish motive" for the incident. He said that the court could not ignore O'Connel's "lifetime of responsible citizenship," which was marred only by a conviction twenty years before for keeping his sons out of school. The courtroom frequently errrupted in laughter and had to be brought to order after the judge remarked the "curious promise of children" which the defendant had repeatedly made to the plaintive.

O'Connel was fined two hundred dollars. He now lives with his youngest son in a trailer near McCarthy's Corner. Having lost his job with Amway, he continues to work part-time in the sales field.

Spice Cake

I was up to my elbows in bacon grease when Sister Celia brought me the news of Frank's death. She didn't look at me when she delivered the blow, just stood there fingering the bacon trays I'd scrubbed and stacked neatly on the garburator: "Frank died last night. You'd better wash these again." Her eyes skittered, her face elongated in a nun's pucker at the sight of my wrists wreathed by greasy rinse water: "And change that water like a good lad." My pig-in-shit complacency shattered, she fluttered off. Oh, she knew better than anyone what the news of Frank's death would do to me, but like all the other chickenshits jogging around these days she preferred to detour past my little pile.

So I stood there alone in the farthest corner of that hospital's kitchen, water beading on my forearms, rainbows of grease manacling my wrists, fists clenching nothing beneath the slick surface. I stood like that for a long moment before I said, Frank killed himself. And then it was as though a part of me had fallen off. I panicked, tried to salvage *me* from *it*. I turned to the garburator, pushed the bacon trays aside and threw up as I hit the ON button. I then hosed down the garburator, changed the water in the sinks, and rewashed the bacon trays. A good lad, thinking the familiar tasks could save me.

But it's been three weeks now since Frank killed himself, and I've scarcely been outside my bedroom since. And that's not the worst of it. All I can do is lie up here masturbating like a caged monkey, every hour on the hour. I push and pull and choke it till stomach cramps and a dhong like a skin-bursting sausage make it impracticable to do anything else but sleep. As Jonathan Swift translated Rochefoucaualt's maxim:

"In all Distresses of our Friends
We first consult our private Ends."

Ah, but what if you have no private ends? Or, better yet, what if your privates end a bit too close to your body proper? Eh? A mean business that, no? That's what ended Frank. His penis was chopped off. Dhong gone. He couldn't live with it (or *without* it, as he said), without it and with the carelessness of the surgical blundering that led the same surgeon to lob his knob off after (what is in hindsight) the terminally clumsy big toe skingraft. Frank, weasel as he could, couldn't weasel his way out of a crotch like a mannequin's wet dream. (*Popping your weasel*, that's what Frank called jerking off.) But my sight is hindsight.

Right now I'm going through what feels and smells like a nervous breakdown. If I'm lucky—and I'm not—it'll go away before I'm taken away. This evening is the first time I've come clear in days. So, I will grip tighter my leaky ballpoint and continue my story, see where that lands me.

Until recently, I was a compulsively neat person, clean as a white wall, an early riser, only an occasional choker of the one-eyed mole. Now, there is no rug big enough to conceal my mess. Oh, my bed is still perfectly made each day, complete with hospital corners, and my desk looks as though it's been tidied by Freud's private secretary. But that's it for order. The rest of the room is littered with caked Kleenex and adhesive underwear. I sleep sixteen dreamless hours a night, and waken exhausted. Or I dream all night of the same thing: an angular piece of modern sculpture, say, one of those metal things all planes and points that looks like it'd dismember you if you got too close, viewed incessantly in a single-bulb grey room from only one angle, and waken exhausted.

I once read that excessive masturbation is a symptom of emotional disorder. It's true! I've forsaken Kleenex and underwear. There isn't the paper potential in the forests of Canada to contain the symptoms of *my* disorder! . . . I will surely pull it off. Literally I mean.

Hindsight: I'd be working right now and Frank would be alive if I'd fixed it so he'd remained potwasher. You see, I was flushed out of my potwasher's alcove when Frank joined the kitchen boys. I was promoted to Nun's Helper, nun's number one boy, which is as high as you can go on the nun's side. . . . But I need to look a little further back to explain it clearly. On the boys' side, where they load the food on a conveyor belt and clean up after meals, you can rise through four levels, from silverware—big spoon, little spoon, knife, fork—to tray-scraper on clean up, each promotion bringing greater responsibility, which means closer contact with Sister Celia. Scraping trays is a job that requires more speed than I command. Food carts were backed up into Emergency when I tried scraping and stacking dishes for the conveyor-belt washer. But there was more to my ineptness than simple clumsiness. I couldn't stand the noise and confusion on the boys' side, the practical jokes, the dirty jokes, the cut-down jokes. So I probably messed-up subconsciously. I was brought over to the nun's side and set to work on pots.

Frank was hired to wash pots and I was promoted to Nun's Helper when Charlie joined the Canadian Armed Forces (or, as the boys called our own fighting Jack-offs, "the Canadian Armed Foreskins"). Quit her, after five years of *her* devoted training, her own Charlie, Sister Celia complained to inanimate objects. She couldn't understand that poor Charlie had to leave, that five years of close quarters with her and five years of eating lunch with the coven up in the nun's quarters was turning him into a nun. You could hear it in the way he clucked his tongue and see it in his hand going for the phantom crucifix on his chest when the boys were horsing around. I guess poor Charlie figured that the Army could remake him into a man, that there the other guys might even call him Chuck, unlike our kitchen troops who called him "Fuckface."

Frank was hired to wash pots, but it wasn't long before he'd weaseled his way into Celia's good graces and I was back on pots. Of course it was inexcusable favouritism, and I despised Frank for being such an ass-kisser. But Frank also has (or had, I guess) a way with men, for he soon weaseled his way into my good graces. I wish he was here to help me weasel my way out of this stinking depression, to hit me with one our pat fart jokes. But that would take a miracle. Celia would have him canonized the patron saint of pot-washing weasel jerk-offs! St. Francis of Sarnia: The Patron Saint of Weasel-Popping!

To the point. I had been back on pots for a week, and loving it. I could see that Frank was sorry for having weaseled his way into my job as Nun's Helper. He hadn't been in the kitchen long enough to know that working close to the nun was hell. I could feel him sticking his eyes into my potwasher's alcove whenever he had cause to pass my way. I didn't let on I was content, of course, and barely acknowledged his presence when he was forced to ask my help with the huge soup cauldrons. I still thought him an ass-kissing weasel, though I was grateful he'd won the nun's favour. Why? Because I loved my potwasher's job. It is the greatest job in the kitchen. As Frank speedily realized, to his credit, his promotion had served only to spring him out of pots and into the fire.

The potwasher's alcove is the most underrated corner of St. Stephen's Hospital (maybe the janitors' corner of the lower-base-ment boiler room compares, but I doubt it). The boys look down on the potwasher's job because it's usually assigned to the lowest boy on the kitchen totem, but the job is simple and the area can be efficiently maintained. Moreover, the area is isolated and quiet. And it is hardly ever graced by the nun.

My initial dislike of Frank came not because of his weaseling character but because his hiring flushed me from my alcove. You see, new boys are usually assigned to silverware. It's only when they can't cut it on the boys' side that Celia brings them to her side and puts them on pots. If they can't cut it on pots, it's either a transfer to the laundry or out the back door. But in Frank's case, Sister Celia couldn't resist the temptation to make an exception to her own rule. ("Temptation," she always snivels, reaching for a left-over dessert, "the one thing I can't resist." Yeah, you and that scrotum scout, Oscar Wilde. I read, Sister, I read.) No, Celia couldn't let that silver-tongued, auburn-haired "lad" get away to the boys. (The nun, who's been in Canada all her unnatural days, does a stage-Irish washerwoman that would put the heart across St. Patrick. . . . But then, he wasn't Irish either.) *Mais non*, Celia couldn't have Monsieur Weasel tugging at her harp strings from the desert of the boys' side. She had to have him on her side, soon to be number one boy by her side. No doubt she foresaw it all in one rosy flash, a gracious intervention of Providence. So, when Charlie quit, she hired Frank to wash pots and promoted me to Nun's Helper.

I was the worst Nun's Helper who ever donned whites. The witch breathed more sugars, shoots, and fudges at my blundering than her Confessor could ever before have countenanced. Of course the witch had subconscious motives (the nun is *all* subconscious). An impeccable performance would have been dismissed as incompetent, such was her crony's desire for the curly head sweating over the bacon trays and pots in the far corner. Anyway, I *was* incompetent. My heart remained in the potwasher's alcove.

One Saturday morning, just as I was hoisting the stacked sausage trays to carry back to Frank, she spoke to a half-plucked chicken: "Now why don't you stay back there and help wee Frank with all those greasy trays like a good gasson." And I knew I was home-free again. So thrilled was I that, under the strain of it all— the load of trays, the news—a wee fart escaped my vigilance; of course the nun would never acknowledge such a sound . But a good *what?* Had she called me a good *asshole?* Were my displaced senses playing tricks?

She came back about an hour later and stood behind us: "You, whatsyourname?" We both turned, though I knew she wanted Frank. "*Moi?*" grinned Frank pointing at his chest. "You," she grunted (and the nun does grunt), "come and give me hand with the Fathers' supper." She pivoted and swished away, just like a nun, a fluttering pain in the ass. I turned to the sinks but watched

Frank dog her steps. Halleluiah! I was reinstated in the nun's limbo, my own heaven, my holy alcove.

I set about reorganizing my alcove, and it was all I could manage during my break and lunch hour to reclaim orderliness from Frank's chaos. I washed the ceiling, the wall, scoured the sinks and the garburator. I emptied the shelves that form a corner behind my alcove and restocked them with supplies from the storeroom, thereby erecting a nun-proof wall. On my knees I scrubbed the floor, and gave thanks. My alcove was a recluse's dream by the time I finished the supper pots that Saturday. Hidden in my chair by my little white table, I was drinking a cup of coffee when Frank intruded.

"Well," he sighed, wiping his hands on his bloodied apron, "that Sister Celia is some old taskmaster."

I slurped insouciantly.

"No shit," he said, snorting about at my improvements. "My, my," mock-awe. "She really gets pissed off, even when you make her laugh. Like when I made her laugh with the plucked chicken. It was like I'd upset her, or something." He was drumming his fingers on my white wall. "What gives around here?"

I ignored him. I merely glanced up with a look that said, Bugger off. I maintained my neutrality, afraid that any hint of agreement would be reported to the nun. He pulled up one of the boxes I'd stacked neatly by the garburator and sat down. He lit a cigarette. I noted that he'd stained my walls with chicken blood.

"You're not supposed to smoke," I snapped.

"Easy lad. *Lad*? What the hell am I saying? God she wears on you awful quick. Shit, next thing she'll have me acting like that Charlie guy she's always going on about. Was he a turd burglar or what?"

He offered me a cigarette. Awed by his irreverence, I took it.

"Hey, you're not pissed off at me for *taking* your job, eh?"

"Forget it," I said, standing. "Well, I must go." It killed me, leaving him smoking in my alcove. I didn't bother changing in the boys' dressing room. I went straight out the back door, straight home, straight up to my bedroom, and locked the door.

The next day was Bacon Sunday. When I arrived in the kitchen, Frank was in my alcove working on the trays. It was like a scene from a spacey update of *The Sorcerer's Apprentice*: some trays were standing half-in half-out of the rinse sink like rockets about to go off, some were scattered about the floor like cowardly soldiers playing dead, some were upside-down and dripping grease from the garburator like the slaughtered mechanical enemy. I stood in the doorway tying the white cap around my head and manoeuvring to see through the gaping holes in my alcove shelves, paranoia pushing panic at the thought that Celia had changed her opinion of Frank and reassigned him to pots. Such a nun-like shift would explain his irreverence the night before. But then she looked up from the sliced peaches she was arranging: "Be a good lad and tell Franky to come and help me with the Sisters' lunch."

Franky! I skipped back to my alcove.

"She says for you to go and help her with the nuns' lunch."

"Oh God no, not up there again." He spun around, pressed his arms to the sinks behind and did a pretty good James Cagney: "You're the one, you rat, you dirty rat." He dried his hands on *my* apron and spoke normally: "Was that her idea or yours?"

"C'mon, Frank. She likes you." I was uncharacteristically and unnaturally gleeful and ironic. "Now you go and help her bring the wee cart up to the wee leper colony. Sit up there and have a tasty wee bite. Make some joke with the cucumber and the peaches. They'll love you, it'll be fun!" I'd no sooner spoken so than I thought I'd gone too far.

"Prick," was all he said, and he left, smiling for inscrutable reasons.

I cleaned up the mess and had my alcove back in order before Frank reappeared dressed in clean whites and pushing the cart of delicacies towards the elevator that was the only access to the nun's quarters. With her head bowed, Celia wheezed from the tail of their tiny procession, "Now you mind the store like a good lad while Franky and meself have our wee bite with the Sisters." Wee bite my ass. I saw his eyes close and his lips compress. I smiled to myself.

It was only eleven-thirty. They wouldn't be back until after one. I changed my apron, procured a pot of coffee, and stole an early lunch at my little white table. After lunch I read *The Sarnia Spectator*. Fantastic: a fifteen-year-old kid was found dead in Our Lady of Mercy Church, possible drug overdose, possible suicide, autopsy to follow. What next? On my second cup of coffee it struck me that I was feeling too smug. I've always disliked feeling too strongly about anything so meaningless, or about anything. I was deriving too much pleasure from Frank's discomfort. Lunching with harpies would be a buffet banquet compared to lunching with the stingy nuns.

Feeling so self-righteous and secure, I felt pampered by my lot in life, and felt like pampering. I walked over to the pastry shelf and scooped out two fingers of whipping cream, licked my fingers clean, returned to my table and lit the cigarette Frank had given me the day before. I decided I'd be friendlier to Frank, a monumental decision for me. I'd never had a friend, not that I couldn't have had as many as I wanted. It's just that I prefer to keep things simple, my priorities in order, my friendly feelings for numero uno. I've never felt any compulsion to prove myself as some sort of I'm-okay-you're-okay wimp. But I figured that Frank disliked and distrusted me because he assumed I'd manipulated his promotion to Nun's Helper. The untidy misunderstanding bothered me. It would be a challenge now to befriend him, and I've always enjoyed meeting a challenge to restore order to my well-ordered life. Besides, I loved the way the nun didn't know what to make of him, whether to laugh with him, or at him, or just pack him off to the laundry.

I was finishing off the lunch pots when Frank came back with a pot of coffee and a few slices of spice cake. He sat at my table, poured a cup of coffee, and already had eaten a piece of cake before he deigned to address me.

"She says for us to take a break."

"I want, to finish, here, first." I couldn't stand the idea of his sharing my alcove. Knob-gobbling Charlie had always taken his breaks alone in the hospital's coffee shop.

"God, you should've seen the way they were competing with each other upstairs. 'No, Sister, I've eaten far too many sweets lately, and what with Lent upon us again. You have another piece of Sister Celia's scrumptious spice cake.' 'Oh, but Sister, you know that I couldn't possibly have *two* pieces' (the first nun, a big one, had just inhaled her third piece), 'especially when I think of all those starving children in Africa.' 'Quite right, Sister. But as Our Saviour said, we will *always* have them with us.' They tee-heed, then the big one took another piece. Really, we're lucky to come away with these crumbs. Come on, take a break already, you can get those later."

I almost laughed out loud at his impersonations, in spite of myself. I'd seen enough of it, the way the nuns—well, it's not just the nuns—the way people can be so selfish. Nonetheless I snapped, "Take a break yourself!" And ooh boy, I'll tell ya, the old cock-swallowing Charlie I heard in my voice put the St. Celia heart across me meself. It was all I could do to continue washing, wishing he'd finish his coffee and *leave me alone*.

He started sniffing, slightly at first as though he didn't intend me to hear, but it grew louder: "Hoo-whee! Did you fart?"

I spun and caught him staring disgustedly at me, his hand over his nose and mouth. "No, I didn't," I all but squealed, stupidly appalled at the thought of anyone, especially this intruder, accusing me of farting in *my* alcove. I turned to my sinks and plunged my hands into the rainbowed water, hoping that the hysterical edge to my voice might be taken for shocked indignation.

"Well then ... would you please?" He asked so timidly, so trustingly, like a child who comes from the bathroom and asks any acquaintance to do up his fly.

I went rigid. I vibrated, as must the piano wire when the true tuning fork is tapped. Small concentric waves radiated from my taut wrists. My eyes clouded and I started gulping short breaths, like a kid who's unable to tear a wholesome cry from his lungs. And I started to laugh. At myself with Frank with and at myself and Frank. I looked at him sitting smugly, so sure of himself in my alcove, another piece of the spice cake heading for his slightly twisted mouth. I started to howl. It was the first time I'd had a howling fit since I was a kid. It was short lived.

Frank stuffed a piece of spice cake into my mouth and clamped it shut with one hand on top of my head and the other under my chin á là Moe on Curly. I managed to swallow dryly. He pulled me to the table and poured a cup of coffee: "Quiet down or Celia'll have our balls." Prophetic Frank.

We became good friends after that. I helped Frank to some serious literature; he had me reading the advice column in *Penthouse*. I took him to a showing of Fellini's "Casanova" at Lambton College; he took me to my first dance, where he picked up two girls for us, where for the first time I felt two real breasts pressing against me like prods with some give to them. The fart joke became our password. Instead of saying hello when we met, we pretended to be strangers and publicly accused each other of having farted. We anticipated our responses to situations where other people accused us of having farted, or where others farted and then tried to deny it. We grew adept at performing improvisationally.

Yes, we became the kind of good friends that guys rarely are. Young women seem to do much better at one-on-one friendship. They hold hands, they hug, they kiss, they trade clothes. It simply never occurs to two guys to trade pants for a day. Girls even sleep over! It's not easy for two guys to be friends like that—not that I ever wanted to do any of *that* with Frank. But girls don't seem to give a second's thought to being called queer. Even when they're small you see pairs of them linked arm-in-arm and sticking out their tongues at the teasing jealous world. Guys manage that only in packs, like jackals. And who knows, maybe deep friendship between two people depends on physical contact. But I don't know anything any more. Anyway, Frank and I, we had the fart joke.

Sorry. This is beginning to sound like tough-guy shit: "Anyways, Franky and me, we had the fart joke." Let me pick it up.

I still thought the funniest fart joke was Frank's original, so I tried to set it up on a girl, one of a delicious pair Frank had picked up for us. She was sitting with me in Canatara Park beneath the silver leaves of a birch tree, her arms clasping her drawn-up knees. It was early Spring, there was a damp chill in the evening air. The moment sure felt right, like romantic scenes I'd only read and dreamt about, and I hoped the fart joke would loosen her up (she seemed to be having trouble accepting that she was with me, not Frank). But when I asked her if she'd farted she turned red, jumped up and ran back into Rose Gardens, where I lost her in the crowd of roller-skaters. I learned from Frank the next day that his girl had told him all about it, that (as these things always turn out for me) the girl I'd asked actually had just let an SBD fart—silent but deadly. That's when Frank explained that I didn't even have the style to handle the sort of woman whose health is determined by the temperature of her nose. "That's what comes from reading so much," he shouted. "Musclebound!" he pointed at his head. "You're like the weightlifter who rams the icecream cone into his fucking nose!" Good friends, but competitive.

I never did have occasion to the use the original fart joke that Frank had pulled on me. Irrationally I grew determined to think up a better joke, one as simple and to the heart. But I never came close to achieving the results he'd wrung from me. Oh, once we met at the supermarket check-out and he asked me loudly and disgustedly if I'd farted, and I said, "Why yes, sir, but not half so well as my friend can." And he'd laughed for a good while. Still, that wasn't nearly enough. I wanted something that would make him crack up completely, a fart joke that would blow him away, that would make him kill himself trying not to howl too loudly, the way he had overpowered me with his, "Well then . . . would you please?" What I wanted, I suppose (I'll confess), was something that would make him—Come on, out with it! Off with it!—*die* laughing.

(Have I said that I'm depressed? Yes?)

The last Bacon Sunday that Frank worked, the nun, who'd begun to dislike, distrust, and confuse him with me, had the whip on his back and her tongue wet-toweling his ass. If I hadn't been humming (an oddity) in the security of the white-tiled resonant alcove, I would have sworn that it *was* me and not her latest ex-pet who was bearing the white boys' burden. In fact, Frank once had to say quite loudly, "I'm Frank, Sister. *Frank.*"

At about three that afternoon he came to the entrance of the alcove, red in the face, the sides of his white shirt soaked with sweat. Without giving our password—"Did you fart?"—he told me to come and help put the soup cauldron in the freezer.

"You look run ragged," I said, drying my hands on his apron.

"I can't take her anymore," he said, for no good reason turning his face to the wall. "All of a sudden she *hates* me. I'm gonna quit. Who needs it?"

I wanted to shout my answer, but I hung back as he walked ahead to the huge soup cauldron. I could tell from the greasy yellow film on the surface that it was Celia's watery chicken broth, a cauldron of broth as least three feet in diameter. Frank bent over, took one of the handles and looked up at me: "Well, come on, give me hand." I stepped back and pretended to applaud. Stupid, I know. Frank looked at me disgustedly. I felt pincers grip the scruff of my neck in the meanest pinch.

Frank shook his head and squatted. With his knees bracketing the cauldron, he tried to straighten his legs but managed to lift it only an inch or so off the floor. A fart squealed out like a runty piglet. His head snapped back, and with the cauldron still held off the floor he tried to snarl but barely wheezed, "Yes, I farted."

I stepped forward and held out my hand: "In that case, may I join you, my friend?" and farted sympathetically, loudly, and, thanks to the tiled kitchen, resoundingly.

Frank's chest caved in as a blast of snot shot from his nose into the broth. He dropped the cauldron and screamed. I don't know where I found the strength, but I grabbed one handle and tossed the cauldron about a yard away. It made a *bung* sound like a muted bell and a pool of bilish broth washed across the floor's red tiles, under the steel pressure cookers, and across Sister Celia's white orthopedic ankle boots, splashing up on what I could see of her thick white-stockinged calves. Frank's right foot looked like a piece of crushed cherry pie in his once-white sneaker.

I waited at the hospital until late that evening. Every half-hour Celia came into the waiting room to ask about Frank and to remind me that I should never have let him carry such a burden by himself. Her vainly bleached moustache seemed to bristle and her counterfeit brogue came even thicker as she stood fingering her crucifix, complaining what a load it was to have to make up a new "crock" of broth without the help of her "wee Franky himself." She brooded aloud on the fate of her accident-free record. "Sure and it'll be hot around here when that ould safety inspector gets wind of our wee mishap." A doctor finally came and told me that he had been able to save Frank's foot but that the big toe had been amputated. "Could be worse," he remarked breezily. Everyone's a prophet.

I visited Frank every day the following week. I brought magazines:*Playboy, Harper's, The Atlantic Monthly, Penthouse, Saturday Night, Knave, Hustler* (which I had to pick up in Port Huron and smuggle across the border), *The New Yorker,* and the equally cosmopolitan *Big Apples.* Frank read all with equal interest, shifting smoothly from one mauve-coloured piece of pretense called *Canadian Poetry* to a bent-eared rag in which a woman confesses that her fantasy since puberty has been to have Lord Byron "do things to me in the rare-books room" of the lost Alexandrian library. I remarked that Byron made out very well with a club foot. Every day Frank complained about a pain in his big toe and a burning itch in his cock. Every day I explained that the former was a phantom pain, the latter a fantasizer's. We laughed a lot during these visits. We made a point each day of having at least one new fart joke, and we often laughed again at the line that had caused him to drop the cauldron. "It was almost worth the big toe," he joked.

In my potwasher's job I resumed my old ways, keeping quiet in my alcove with my shelves well stocked, hoarding jokes for Frank's return.

At the end of the first week of Frank's convalescence, his doctor discovered that gangrene had invaded the penis. During the skin-graft operation, while removing a layer of skin from the inner thigh with an instrument that resembles a razor-sharp cheese slicer, this same doctor had pricked the head of the penis. The nurses who'd been changing the dressing on Frank's big toe either had not noticed when they checked the thigh or had chosen to ignore Frank's "fantasizer's pains." That Saturday afternoon, a good chunk of the penis was removed.

It's true what they say about seeming content before suicide (though I see now that Frank's contentment was resignation, that the difference between contentment and resignation is in the laugh). Frank appeared content the last time I visited, the day before he was released from that hospital, the day before he killed himself—the first time I'd bothered to visit since the crucial removal. He was reading *Harper's* magazine (had it hidden behind a *Penthouse*) when I stuck my head into his private room, actually stuck my head in, sniffed wincingly, and demanded, "Did you fart?"

He looked up from his reading with the phoniest grin and the emptiest eyes I've ever seen: "No, I always smell this way."

It was an answer I'd used once before. Repetition was taboo. I should have known right then that something was seriously wrong. But then I noticed, or imagined, that the room did have a bad smell. When Frank saw that suspicion on my face he frowned, putting a stop to the beginnings of my, "Sorry I—"

"Why, did you fart?" he countered.

That took me off guard. I smiled down at the bag I was carrying and headed for the bedside chair. I sat and rigidly removed my gaze from the doubled magazines that lay open on his crotch. I skirted his eyes and looked at the asexual Sacred Heart hanging at the head of his bed: Jesus pointing to his bleeding heart, thorns like sutures crowning the frighteningly exposed organ. I met those eternally accusing eyes for a moment.

I remembered my joke: "No, I didn't." I tried to act as indignant as I'd been that first time in the kitchen. Then complaisantly, "Would you like me to?"

That broke him up. I was thrilled.

I flipped through his *Penthouse* and we laughed at his lingering concern over being caught with a magazine that contained anything but naked women and puerile humour. He boasted that he had a reputation to uphold. He acted so naturally it never occurred to me that I was discussing sex with a eunuch, though he wasn't technically a eunuch. (Is there a word for what happened to Frank? *Penilized?*) He didn't seem to notice this irony either, didn't behave at all like an emasculated man, except for the occasional hollowness of his laugh.

I presented my gift. He took the new book out of the brown bag and read the title aloud: *"The Sun Also Rises.* Very biblical."

"You've read the bible?"

"Uh, duh, yeah, the one with big printing and coloured pictures. Fuck off. What's the book about?"

"A man," I blurted, "who has his works ruined in a war and learns to live with it."

"Don't you mean, *without it? . . .* And the sun cometh no more."

I laughed too loudly, cackled the way Celia did when Frank pretended that a turkey neck was trying to fly from her cleaver. I let my laughter die when I saw that Frank was just staring at me.

"Besides," he said, "the sun doesn't rise. Maybe he should have called it *As The World Turns.* Sounds sort of soapy to me."

I snorted appropriately. A rough beginning, but we were soon talking like old times. No further reference to the butt, stub, scar, mutilation, or whatever there was where his penis once hung. At one point things got a little quiet and my gaze drifted back to the pathetic picture of Jesus, and I said just for something to say, "What do you think Jesus would have been like as an old man?"

Frank furrowed like I was pulling a trick question on him: "I don't know. Why you askin' me? Probably still talking about the tricks he used to do but can't do any more. Who gives a shit."

"Well don't get all wrangy about it. I was just wondering."

He snorted, smiled, moved his hand and almost touched me: "Yeah, right, well you're gonna just have to keep wonderin', Nun's boy."

"*Nun's boy!* "

"Nothing man."

And we both had one good last laugh.

My last image of Frank has him reading the biographical sketch of Hemingway on the book's jacket. It's no wonder the detectives gaped at me in disbelief, and then with open contempt, when I explained about that book.

The detectives also told me how Frank killed himself, *after* they'd taken down the implicating facts. (I know they'd like to blame me for his death, if only to covertly exonerate the doctor, the hospital staff, and Sister Celia.) I confessed that Frank had once told me his father kept a handgun in a shoe box in the parents' bedroom closet. Frank said the last time he'd seen the gun, his father was drunkenly wielding it about at a New Year's Eve party. It certainly looked and felt like the genuine article, but then neither of us had ever handled a real gun before.

The detectives told me that Frank had taken the gun down to the basement, sat behind the furnace, put the barrel inside his mouth (apparently, they pointed out, until it touched the back of his throat), and pulled the trigger. But it wasn't a real gun. It was a prop, the sort that shoots out a stick with **POP!** printed on a piece of cloth. The stick had shot down Frank's throat. The cause of death was asphyxiation. He had suffocated in his own vomit.

When they told me that, amid the comfort and orderliness of my room, I had my second convulsive howling fit since childhood. There being no Frank and spice cake handy, the detectives had to call a doctor to sedate me. That was when all this began, and I've not been out of this dump since. Even now when I let myself think of it I suffer a fit of giggles. I'm sure, you see, that Frank knew exactly what he was doing. That he did it to get even with me. Suicide by prop. Jesus!

But I shouldn't have walked out on Celia after she brought me the news of Frank's death. I was made to be a potwasher, a nun's boy nothing man. Not that I believe that one book had anything to do with his suicide. No, I doubt Frank even bothered to read anything but the biographical sketch. It's that me as potwasher—my holy alcove—did have something to do with the chain of events that led to the suicide. Me as the snivelling tail-between-the-legs nun's boy who complacently let Frank weasel his way up to Nun's Helper. And now I've been flushed out of my alcove for good. Some good. Or I have exchanged alcove for bedroom, this room that is part-chaos part-order.

Should I upturn my desk, mess up my bed, and jerk of again? Or should I pop out and join the joggers who trot past my window with the regularity of my self-abusings? Is that what Frank would have me do? . . . But they're not joggers, they're running shit-dodgers, panting past with that resigned look of pained prey being stalked by a plodding ineludible beast.

What's that joke?

May I join you, my friend?

Why?

Because I'm coming apart.

Rounded With A Sleep

Today turned out a grand day, certainly better than most . . . if I don't think back too far. Let's just say it was better than yesterday and leave it at that. My bitching got Flo back at last. Flo's not her real name, nor Florence neither for that matter. Her real name's Betty, *Big* Betty when she starts getting pushy. I call her Flo because she looks a bit like that Southern waitress that used to be on the TV show. She's my nurse, too, so it's a fair joke. And Flo likes a joke. She's a good six foot and a hundred and eighty pounds, with a breadth of arse on her like a sow's and a stack of straw-coloured hair like an overloaded hayrick. She always wears her nursing-school pin stuck in her hair like a pitchfork, and she's got the devil in her. So that's another fair joke. I've got the cancer in me—but no call to be feeling sorry. I've lived long enough and caused enough mischief. And like I said, I'm feeling no pain after today. Though that could be worse, I suppose. Maybe when I slip off tonight I won't be back. . . . Ah, but that's all right too, because then I'll be with my Alice. Sure. After a spell in purgatory, of course. And maybe with Mary too. Who knows.

I don't know either who it was made Flo what she is, or if anyone did. I just thank God. Nor do I know who it was invented the drug cocktail they feed us here, but I thank God for him too. Dulls the pain and leaves my mind clear.

And I don't know who the hell it was wrote that book about dying, but I regret the day she picked up a pen. Some German woman. Her name sounds like the cookie elves on the TV commercial. Cobbler, or some such. Well intentioned, I suppose, but surely half-arsed off her rocker. My youngest girl, Elizabeth (a big sop of a thing, pushy and mushy—but I love her, I love her), she made me promise I'd read the book. Which I did, some anyway. I've read only two books through in my entire life, the Bible and *Piers Plowman* (Mary tricked me by saying it was the first book on farming). After them two I don't see why you need bother with any others.

Be that as it may, that dying book's made it so *I* can't die in peace. The whole family's read it. All but Owen, my youngest boy, who thinks he knows everything already. Or did till he found that life can take you by the heels and shake the conceit out of you. There now, I'm your death-bed philosopher. But I guess I know some things.

One thing is this: The world's a mess, and the things we might use to make it right are the very things that've messed it up.

Here's another: The thing that makes people wonderful is the way they're driven to come together—this also dooms us.

And here: Talk is a kind of sickness.

When I opened my eyes this morning, my eldest boy, David, was standing at the foot of the bed. His tribe, all six of them, were cavorting all over the room like the Jews impatient for Moses to come down from Sinai. David and Marge claim the kids are being exposed to the *idea* of death. I'll say they are. So familiar they've grown, you might say they're bored to tears with the whole business of my dying. Their conniptions near drove me to expose *them* to a nearer familiarity themselves right then and there. But have you ever heard the likes? The *idea* of death. Now, I really *don't* want to come across as some kind of potato Plato (that's a name Mary had for me), but it seems to me that *idea* doesn't rightly hit the nail on the head. I mean, it's not like death's something *we* thought up.

As David's Marge was out getting coffee, Flo took command. "Kids, come with me and I'll take you to a room where there's Space Invaders."

"Space Invaders!" shouted Stevie, their youngest.

"That old game's *boring*," sneered Willy, at twelve their oldest, and named for me. Poor fella, till then he'd been quiet, struggling to behave grown up. "Don't you have *Airheads?*"

Ignoring him Flo winked at me (and there's not many a woman can wink, though my Alice could): "Then I'll pack you little space invaders off." Woman's got a way with words, like Mary had. Though Flo's like neither my Alice nor my Mary. She puts me most in mind of my own mother, who seemed so big and. who could be both soft and sharp.

David wanted to put a halt of Flo, with his looking-about, where's-Marge gawk of a face. But the children weren't to be denied.

At the doorway Flo looked back, a mock-worried pout fighting true concern: "Sweetheart, how are you feeling this morning?"

"I'll live, love, I'll live." Though I had to fight a hacking fit to say it.

"No more cramps, no more stiffness? Tell me the truth now."

"Only when I think of you, love."

She laughed like a smothered sneeze and stepped aside to let Marge into the room. Only two coffees, wouldn't you know it. And God forbid I should ask David or Marge for a smoke again.

"I'll be back with your breakfast in a jiff, lover."

"Not much, Betty. My belly does still feel like there's a sock in my throat." I don't like to call her Flo in front of the others, 'cause it's plain to see David and Marge don't like the dovey way we talk to each other. Marge once said Flo was "unprofessional," like she was a hooker in love or Gretzky gone on a girl.

The son and his wife stood conspiring over the regular red rose Marge was substituting for yesterday's. David's a big man, like I was, same stork's legs and barrel body, same horseface and shock of sandy hair, and same need for a patient woman. Unlike me David was wild for the women when he was young, and unlike me he settled down when he married. So maybe it is best to get it all out of your system. Unlike my Alice, Marge is strong on top of patient. But she's a beauty like my Alice was, same high-riding rounded arse like two snooker cherries snug in a corner, beauts of tits, hair blue-black like rain on a raven, and her face one of those few things that can truly make me regret I'm dying.

Aa, but I knew what David and Marge were whispering: Has he reached Acceptance yet?

I love them—I have to don't I, they're mine—but Goddamn it they're going to drive me to an early grave with the hopscotch way they treat my dying! . . . Early grave? God forgive me.

"Dad?" said Marge.

I knew she was leaning over me, her hand on my shoulder. She didn't have to shake me. God Almighty but I hate that daydreaming! It's them cursed drugs! Cocktail my arse! They're unnatural! Sheer mortification! . . . It embarrasses me.

"Dad?" she said again, as though I'd not heard her the first time. She looked over her shoulder for David: Dave, he's gone! He's clear leapfrogged Acceptance and gone!

"Yes, darling, I was just thinking to myself."

"Uh, what were you thinking about, Dad?" David asked.

Now that's a question I recognized as straight from the death book, or if not that exact question, the way of humouring. But I had to humour them, had to control myself and remember it wasn't Owen or Margaret. If I'd said what I was thinking, poor David and Marge would've been sorely disappointed, thought I'd slipped clear back to Anger. So I recollected where I was supposed to be. "I was just wondering, son, if you'd get a fair price for the whiteface. What with people knowing we've gotta sell and all."

The way they brightened, it was like when I used to be inside mucking out the stable of a rainy day and suddenly sunlight like a magician's swords would come shafting through every chink in the boards. I'd straighten, close my eyes and fill my lungs slowly through my nose till I felt fit to burst. Such a stab of pure senseless love in my chest that it hurt. And no object for it, not even myself.

"Oh Daddy!" beamed Marge. And any innocent lies I've been tellin'—almost any hurt I've given to Alice and Mary—were worth that beam of a smile. I'll take my time in purgatory. "Of *course* we will. Everyone knows what a conscientious farmer you were—*are*. Callaghan's already said he'll top any bid for the herefords."

"Callaghan! Has he now? Why he's a foot in the grave himself!"

"Now, now, Dad," soothed Marge. "You put your mind at rest on that account. We'll get a great *bargain*."

That's the word, dear. "That's all I want," said I, "a fair price while I've time." Now, what the hell comes after Bargaining?

Marge leaned down and kissed me, one great nipple hard with the excitement of it all and drilling the back of my hand. In the manner I've been relating everything lately, I thought it a bit unfair to be dying now that women have stopped wearing brassieres and started wearing short skirts again. I'm not like that covetous hooer, Callaghan, who pretends it's shameful but can't keep his eyes in his head.

David was as excited as Marge, waltzing about the room, arms waving like he was conducting an invisible choir of angels, chattering on about the great *bargains* he was getting for all that's mine, *was* mine. (You can say it, Marge dear.) Bargain this and bargain that. The way they've cleaned up and pigeon-holed my dying is as bad as the old way of hushing it up. God have mercy on them, and me. Help me forgive Owen for selling off the barn in bits and pieces. Help Margaret with Owen like You helped Alice with me.

Flo came back with my juice and tea and a metal-covered plate that balled the sock in my throat. (Though it could have been my simp's heart, the things seeing my grown married kids so content can do to me yet.) She told David and Marge they'd best leave me rest a while. They must have bruised my fading skin the way they hugged and kissed me. Me lying there like a balded pipe cleaner sunk in a bed of damp cotton.

But don't kid yourself, 'cause I'm not kidding myself; the false oak door had not whooshed tight behind them when I heard David all but shout: "I told you he's the type that'd combine Bargaining and Acceptance!"

The door thudded softly shut, much as I imagine the lid will. They were satisfied with themselves, and me. I was pleased to have been able to do that small turn for them. He's a good son, David, never gave me any serious cause for concern. People say Owen's the image of me, but I can't see it. He's built too close to the ground.

For all that, I'll bargain my puckered arsehole there's no such thing as Acceptance! For the love of all that makes life worth living, I've not yet learned to accept my Alice's death. So much was left unsettled. And hers was a good death, too, as these things go. I've seen bad ones, believe you me . . . one anyway.

I sat up two nights with Mary when she passed on. She was our neighbour. Taught all my kids at the old third-concession school. People who came to the house to pay their respects, as people did then, remarked how peaceful Mary looked, with her hair spread on the pillow as white and scarce as a half-blown dandelion clock. But what do people know.

I'd thought if I sat with her we might talk about God and things, as we used to when I'd go against Alice and help her thrash and bring in her bit of hay, when her hair was the colour of ripe wheat, and her body smelled sweaty sweet and showed through the print dress. She wouldn't wear a man's coveralls for work like Alice did. A real educated lady, Mary. Yet she spend her last twelve hours cursing God for leaving her with nothing—no husband, no children. She raved at me, about me, welcomed death, even hell. God forgive her, and me. But I could never leave Alice, who hated me after Mary died.

I've hated myself a lot longer. The plain truth is, I've never sorted it out. You see, I could talk to Mary about things, God and the like, though mostly about myself. And she was genuinely interested. But I loved Alice. Though I've never been settled in my own mind if it was a failure of nerve or if I loved Alice *that* much. At times it was like walking about with a wedge driven into my head. If it'd been possible, I'd have split myself in half the way Solomon wanted the baby.

There'd been no remarks for a while about how I'd been spending so much of my time, no hint of the old contrariness. When it was rain for sure, Alice skipped making lunch and came out to work alongside me. Time was tight, the day grew close, and it was getting on to supper. Then the hayrick cracked it's last good bearing. As we were doing a lickety-split fix, Alice let the bed slip and just nipped my thumb. I cursed a blue streak, said why didn't she stay in the house and read and get some goddamned brains in her head! She didn't get mad, just pried up the bed and talked polite-like to me for three years, then died. And this happened after Mary died. We were both sixty-seven. There's immortality of a kind for yeh.

Flo set up my breakfast, mischief in her eye and her rear sort of humped back for fear I'd make a grab. Maybe it was the feel of Marge's breast had settled me like a she-goat put in with a stallion, but I didn't have the gumption to lay a hand on Flo's reassuring flesh. That woke the fright in me. I made to brush the steel-covered plate away.

"Uh-uh," sang Flo, tippy-toeing backwards.

"Flo, love, I'm afraid this may be the day." God damn me anyway for the child I am!

"Oh you, you'll say anything for a feel, won't you, bad boy?"

I don't mind much when Flo babies me. My guess is she babies everyone, dying or not. Though they're not supposed to treat us like that here. "It's not that unflagged wide load behind you, it's them runny scrambled eggs I know are under there. Take them away with yeh." The image of the soppy eggs in yellow water like pig's piss had me fit to vomit.

"Presto-changeo!" said Flo and whipped off the metal cover.

There on the centre of the dug-brown plate, like Moses' rod Aaron flung down, lay something these tired eyes hadn't set sight on for a week—one glorious unfiltered Players cigarette! Lord, thought I, let what's left of my lungs go to the devil. But I saw it was all the angel's job was worth to be caught, so as she darted glances at the door, I feebly raised my left hand, then like a striking cobra goosed her dead on the dungshoot.

"You dirty old goat! I'll have the, uh . . . the circumcision doctor come up and *fix* you!"

But she loved it. I could see genuine pleasure in the rose tint rising about her throat. Not that I kid myself, mind you. No woman but she's a connivin' hooer likes that sort of treatment. Flo was happy for *me*. She's showed concern only those few times I'd left the *stage* of ornery horniness. Flo's a good woman, as I've said, but she needs her comfortable image too: "the cocky old codger." She'd used those very words the first time she met me, sort of directing me how to behave before I'd even thought of any funny business. But then, I call her Flo. I'll grant it's an odd state of affairs, but you just can't push mushy with people, especially someone in my condition. No matter what the headshrinkers say, some things are better left unsaid. And whatever the fright gets to be, I'll keep it that way.

"Well, you'd best get him up here on the double." I don't know what poor thing in me said that, but I'll gladly accept more time in purgatory.

"Will Hunt, don't you talk like that." Hands backhand on her hippo's hips, she was dead serious, or at least seriously striking the pose. Who knows. But that was my fault for having been the same.

"And *here*." She was mock-mad now. "Keep this till tonight." She flicked the smoke under the near lip of the plate.

Though the smoke had already improved my day considerably, I still said, "Sometimes I lose my wind entirely this last while, love. And I just sort of fade away. My feet go cold, then my legs, then numb. And there's so much I haven't . . . ."

Aa, I wish to God I'd not carried on like that. Better I'd died first. True or not, the indulgence wasn't near worth the look that drew dear Flo's face like a cow that misses its calf. So go on, plant me in purgatory up to my nose in dung, make me stare into Alice's and Mary's hurt and betrayed eyes for eternity.

Flo's lower lip turned out a touch, then she puckered her lips and spoke in the way one does to a baby: "Feeling sorry for ourselves, are we?"

"Must be, *Big* Betty, must be," said I, fighting like the devil to keep from hacking. I reached down toward my pecker: "If you could just rub where the pain is."

"Tch-tch," she shook her head as though she'd expected no better. "It's no wonder poor Alice went on ahead of you. Oh well, some people've got better things to do than stand here risking their jobs listening to your self-pity. I've already been up on the carpet for those bottles you left lying by the bed. Are you turning *senile* on me?"

She's a wonder that woman, to risk saying such a thing. "Well get out with yeh! Who's keepin' yeh! It's no wonder you've been through two husbands, and you just a girl." Oh, she loved that last part, Flo, pushing fifty if she's a day. "Flauntin' your heap of flesh around a poor sick old man that can't die in peace with the likes of yeh! Sure as the fat's bubbling on Jezebel, you"—but I coughed—"you screwed them"—and held my breath—"screwed them into early graves! Out with yeh!" I began hacking up what felt like bits of rag, probably what's left of my lungs. Flo, bless her soul, turned away ranting to high heaven about the ungrateful old codger. She made me a drug cocktail.

She paused passing the foot of the bed, looked down at her feet, or mine: "We're all sorry and scared, sweetheart, even those of us who've got years ahead of us. Don't be too hard on yourself. No one's lived that hasn't hurt someone. God's forgiving." She touched my toes and hurried out.

And that's why I've fallen in love with Flo: the good lies she tells me for my sake. And she's a bit like my Alice, a bit like Mary, and a lot like I remember my mother. I can talk with her, or not, and it's all the same. She knows all about Alice and Mary.

My kids—God bless them and keep them always—would like me to mosey on according to script, their script, or the one they read in the death book. Through all the *stages,* a staged death of a sort. And at times theirs is a tough bill to fill.

Flo seems to know that there's no such thing as stages. Her ornery-codger-with-his-heart-in-the-right-place is an easier role to play. She's seen too many of us kick like whining old dogs out here in Stratford's Prospero Hospice to complicate the business. An old house on the outside, this kip. Inside a hospital, with all the poking and pills and stink of medicine and death you'd find in any hospital. Only here it can be worse. This is a *hospice*, they don't think twice about looking you dead in the eye and telling you the jig's up. No hope, nothing they can do, period. Though, to be fair, the truth can be a relief too. Who but some useless old pismire like Callaghan, who'll hang on as long as his money's earning interest and there are dirty movies to watch on the VCR, would argue that it's wrong they make no *heroic* efforts to keep you living on like some runt that's gotta go. They don't bring you in till you're right on the doorstep. I've heard that some concerned citizens fear that old people who're a burden on their children might feel pressure to come in before their time. I don't think there's much chance of that. I've not seen much of that in my life, outside of stories about old Indians and one fella I knew who threw himself in front of a gun at Dieppe. And as likely as not, that fella was crazy. I hear they're doing something similar at the other end, I mean for women having babies, birth rooms and the like. Come to think of it, it's women who do it all at both ends. So *hospice* my arse, they should simply call it, The Place Where Women Help You Die. I guess I'd rather be closer to home, it's a two-hour drive from Sarnia for David, Marge and the kids. The drug cocktails help.

There's always one of them young girls in peppermint costumes sitting by my head when I wake up. "Tell me all about your life, Mr. Hunt. I'll bet it's *so* interesting." How much you wanna bet? I'll give you two-to-one. They'll be clapping their thighs together like seals begging tossed smelt, the crotch of their pants stayed as if seen with a stroboscope. ... God forgive me. It's no wonder He's taking me. Maybe Flo *has* got me pegged. ... Be that as it may, I'll take my sight of the veiled heaven here while I still can, come what may. Though God's not so forgiving as Flo thinks, surely He won't throw me straight to the devil. Just another millennium in eternity's halfway house. It was Jesus got us that *bargain*, Flo love. And I've not led that bad a life, please God.

Truth to tell, I've little in the titillating way to tell the candystripers and the headshrinkers researching death. (To get in here, and it's cheap, you've to consent to all manner of guineapigging.) But where's Flo's smoke? . . . No, stay your hand, Will, save what strength you have. You've not a hair left on your head to hold a smoke on your ear. Aa, yes, in my shorts. Jesus H! The mortification of it! Twice the size of my withered dick. And an unfiltered Players at that!

Two drags and I'll put it out for a spell, cough myself fit to think again. The drug cocktails you grow numb to, but the smoke . . . ah, the smoke. After a week, two drags is about all I can handle anyway, thick smoke rushing my lungs like sudden fear, then snaking down every limb, flicking an electric tongue at every burning joint it passes.

My life: I've been a farmer all my life. Alice and me raised six children, five still living. I've loved only one other woman in my life. Though I've been to bed only with Alice. I've been to the pictures twice, both times it wasn't what it was cracked up to be. I'll be buried in the Catholic cemetery. Unless you've got up at four every morning of your adult life, put on the same clothes and stepped out into a cold dark world of never-ending work and money worries, there's nothing more I can tell you that you'd understand. That just happens to be the truth. It probably is for you too.

Heaven would be nice, but I don't really need that dream either. Somewhere deep in my mind and heart I know that God and heaven and hell are but good lies we've dreamed up to keep the conceit out of us here on earth, and to let us live together without killing each other. And for all my talk of purgatory, I'll be content to sleep for eternity, mingle with dung and stardust. Long as there's no bad dreams, none of that head-splitting over Alice and Mary.

I've got off only one really good line since coming here. A smart-alecky doctor at the head of a group of nervous snotnosed nurses asked me boldfaced: "Mr. Hunt, would you please tell our nurse trainees what you think happens to you when you die?"

Said I: "Doctor, I'm still wondering what happened to me when I was born." And the girls laughed.

There, I'd say all that puts me a fairer way near to Acceptance than any of my kids dream.

Light up, Will, you ornery old arsehole. You vain and conceited windbag. Your best notions are ones Mary put in your head and you know it. Ah Mary, imagine me become a "treasure house of experiences."

Alice, I won't die with this between us. I won't die with this between us. I won't die with this between us. I won't die. . . .

Margaret, Owen's wife, was up just after lunch. She comes frequently as she lives only fifteen minutes away; in fact, it was her idea to bring me here. With a drug cocktail and some vegetable soup like dishwater in my belly, and Flo's smoke still to look forward to, I was feeling no pain.

Margaret's not like David's Marge. She never talks about herself. Only Owen, Owen this and Owen that. Owen would have come with her only Massey has him on a short leash. "Owen's got another raise. Owen says you were right, Dad. He told me *expressly* to apologize for the argument yesterday. He should never have sold the barnboard." And to her credit she had to add, "Though he did get more for it in pieces from the antique dealers. Owen's worried about . . . something. Are you still *Angry*, Dad?"

She laughed nervously. She senses what's bothering Owen, yet she loves him madly. And she knew I sensed something too, though I tried not to let on.

"No, dear, I can *Accept* now that he got a good *Bargain*."

She laughed more genuinely. Margaret's not so quick and modern as Marge, so we can kid together about the death book. She's a farm girl, shy and big-boned, though not near so big as Flo. Unlike the girls in my day, she's been to the farming college in Guelph. And shy though she is, she can speak up for herself, and will, when the time comes.

Owen's the only son who married a girl from the country. He went through business at the university in London, then got a top job with the Massey-Ferguson outfit near Tavistock. He married Margaret, his old sweetheart, and settled on a small farm—a big garden really—near Shakespeare. Though Owen's never been settled like David.

"I think he needs to, uh, talk to you about . . . something, Dad."

She didn't want to talk, though. She held up her hand: "No. Please. He'll be up."

I doubted it. He knows what good talk is, like me.

She leaned down to kiss me, changed her mind and rested her cheek on my sparrow's chest. I stroked her hair, the colour of a polished chestnut and the smell of everything alive and growing. I could almost have died peacefully then. I packed her off. No words called for. That's the way.

But Owen did come up by himself about mid-afternoon. He was as fidgety as a sheep about to be shorn. I figured what it was before he spoke. Maybe I've been given second sight, now that I'm near the end.

Though I didn't want to talk about it, I croaked the few lines I've learned. "It's your life, not Margaret's, not mine. It's all up to you what you make of it . . . son." I've always found it difficult to love Owen. And I admitted why to myself, then, lying there like only a voice from a spent body in a scorching bed.

"But I love her too, Dad. . . . I'll be thirty next year."

"Margaret knows, son. Oh maybe not the particulars, but the impression. She's smarter than you give her credit for. She loves you, but she won't be long-suffering."

"I shouldn't be laying all this on you now, Dad, when you're . . ." A choked hiccup like from a burped baby. And did you see the way he pulled back. Or was it something I said?

"Lay it on me, son."

He laughed at that, then pulled back and cried quietly like he was trying to keep a toad from jumping out of his chest. Lord how we do struggle to conceal the real things that move us in our little lives, hide the very things that make life worth living. As if anyone with eyes and a brain doesn't know the minute he looks at you and hears you talk. And how we succeed anyway. It's a greater conundrum than hoping to clean up the world by the same means the mess was made. Like setting a fox to guard the chickens. Yes, but who's guarding the fox? What do the chickens and the fox have in common? They both have to be guarded. Yes, and who is more guarded? . . . That's me—the goddamned Plato of potatoes.

Then Owen surprised me. He did kinda lie down by me, the big businessman a big baby. I put a hand on his shoulder and told him softly as I could that he should think twice before seriously hurting Margaret. No one has that right. Children involved or not, you don't promise something one day and say I've changed my mind the next. You do *that* and you're the only child involved. And I said he should know it was only a choice between which would end up hurting him the less—not to kid himself. And not to draw it out.

He all but shat himself with relief. I'd said something like what he wanted to hear. Maybe what he needed. Embarrassed, he mumbled his thanks and love, gripped my wet hand and left.

Dear Jesus, I didn't know what I was saying there for a while, or who I was talking to any more. I suspect I said two different things. . . . But he was Alice's and mine, the late child we had no right to, who saved us many's the time. Mine, I acknowledge that. My last bargain for a restful night.

The door: "Will?"

"Yes, love."

"Say your prayers, dear. It's lights out. *And no more smoke.*"

A welcome darkness. "Flo . . . good night, love."

Whoosh, thud— like the lid.

So, all-in-all it turned out a grand day, certainly better than most. Good night, Will. If you do dream, I pray they're pleasant. Sentimental, I know, but there you have it.

Things Coming Together

At eighteen Michael and Cathy had overreached each other to agree that *The Wizard of Oz* was the best movie ever made. At twenty-eight they bought a VCR and a tape of *The Wizard*, but in less time than even they'd feared they grew weary of the show and embarrassed by their past fondness. They no longer threw the movie in the faces of friends who enthused about Bergman or Bertolucci. They sold their VCR and their TV and began frequenting a repertory cinema at York University. Michael shot Cathy a mock-alarmed look when she informed a new acquaintance that *The Wizard of Oz* had been shot in black-and-white until Dorothy reached Munchkinland. The friend, a graduate student in what he simply called "film," remarked that it should have been shot the other way around, or simply taken out and shot. When he learned that Michael and Cathy were only six months in Toronto from Sarnia, he moved to another group. Cathy roused Michael in the middle of that night and mocked him for singing a jumbled rendition of "Over the Rainbow" in his sleep.

They agreed before turning thirty not to have children. They were quite content with each other, thank you, and they envisioned no change in what they'd begun calling their "lifestyle." The world had grown such a dangerous place for children. *What* could be more selfish than the animal urge to reproduce themselves, and the seventies seemed such a selfish time to behave selfishly. But thank the gods of fertility that Michael had not gone ahead with the vasectomy. For one whole year before turning thirty-two, they engaged in an unloving sort of sex every third night and recorded each act faithfully and hopefully with little downward-pointing arrows on the Basal Temperature Chart.

Though by thirty-four they had saved enough money to make an impressive down-payment on a modest Toronto house, they remained in the pricey high-rise on Bloor Street. Still childless at thirty-five, and with the frantic coupling now crammed into the three "hot" days of her cycle, Cathy returned full-time to social work. Michael, freer than his family-tied associates in the advertising firm, was promoted to Chief Field Representative, in which capacity he travelled a lot, naturally.

That had appeared to be the end of their story: secure, yet challenging and fulfilling employment, accommodation of a sort to one another's individual lifestyles, a nice place on Bloor. Then Cathy determined again at the age of thirty-seven that she wanted a real home and family. A home like she'd had in Port Lambton.

Michael throws back his Jameson's and, posed like a feeding chick, taps the bottom of the glass. He crunches the ice-cube, tucks a chunk under his tongue, then slurps the rest, or most of it, into the glass. He sucks warm air and wonders: What if she doesn't come back this time? . . . He may as well have another. And with the next swallow again he doesn't care. She could return or fly over the fucking rainbow, he tells himself.

Slowly he circles his elbows forward, and the clammy shirt pulls free from between his shoulder blades. Resting his left elbow on the liquor cabinet she'd given him their first Christmas together, when she thought him a cute drunk, he cups his forehead in his hand and shifts the piece of ice to sit on last week's filling. He winces as when the dentist's pick had probed the rotting tooth, but the twinge proves to be but the true pain's scout. He glances over his shoulder and touches his crotch. The *problem*. That's how he's named her infidelity. A roar as from a sprung incinerator door flushes his face, phases him out.

Cathy circles the display table, bellying away, enticed back, like a thing played patiently on a line. Coward! she admonishes. What makes the muskrat guard his musk? She does love candles, though, the poor woman's fireplace. He'd once bought her a box of a hundred, all the same washy grey of his eyes. Bring *him* a candle . . . a peace offering. Better yet, bring a chamber stick. Let him supply the candle! She shouldn't joke. He's really been good that way since he cut down on the boozing, after she'd read to him that abstinence from all intoxicants helped John Lennon get Yoko pregnant—*how Yoko had gotten pregnant.* And she's a lot older than me. Well, okay, not a lot. But what's she thinking. She should be home for their talk. *Their talk?* Has she sunk to the clichés of TV talk shows?

"May I help you with something?"

"No, just looking."

"If it's the cost of the box that concerns you, we do sell singly."

My coat! My boots! She thinks I'm a goddamned bag lady!

On the stuffy bus she suffers a sudden chill and hugs herself. With her nose—hooked, she planned to have it done after they buy the house—touching the window, she watches an old couple like paired crows. Old men often grow so considerate and contrite, the feminine side that their fathers suppressed surprises near the end like an old woman's facial hair, mocking a life of simple distinctions. True in spades for what I know about Mikey's father. But that's the psychologist speaking. *And* the evader. There are probably just as many mean old buzzards. And Michael's pretty considerate already, anyway. . . . Still, it is touching the way the old boy takes the old girl's elbow at the curb. Mikey could at least have bought me a used car! He's to blame for it with his . . . Be fair, Catherine. You're the one who insisted on living cheaply, on saving for the house, with a fireplace. Save on booze, on eating out, on . . . Oh, who cares any more!

She frowns at a split thumbnail, then sticks it into her mouth and stares at the scraped toes of her boots, her feet freezing in the melting slush from the filthy streets. Who would have predicted such a storm in early October?

She hadn't lied! ... Though the gin that early after last night's wine *had* made her head spin and perhaps had caused her revelation to be more truthful than was called for. If there are degrees of truth.

On the phone that afternoon he'd wailed that he'd never done anything, *honestly!* Then he'd laughed that idiot's cackle. "What a fool," he'd mumbled to be heard as he hung up. But she knew him better than that: he would be as smug yet about his uncompromising fidelity as he'd once been of theirs. (Of course there are degrees of truth. Everything's relative. He's always said so himself.) A trophy, really, like his hollow statue of the little football man. Or no, more like a stuffed dove, that's what she is to him! Or what she had been. Oh, screw it!

She feels the cold wind from the open side door and looks up to find the driver's unshaven face turned toward her. A neatly dressed teenager shouts at a wino and slaps his head: "Get off, you rang the bell!" The wino falls into the aisle, other kids laugh. The driver leaves his seat and with surprising gentleness helps the wino right himself.

She steps down and slush slops over the top of her right boot. She stumbles onto the sidewalk, air brakes hiss, she turns and sees two heavily made-up girls pointing and laughing at her from the back window of the bus. What did I do? Before she has walked a block she is begged for money, asked "How much?" and passed slowly by a police cruiser.

Pain like a white-out blankets Michael's senses, excruciating exit, ecstatic distraction. Sharp pain eases, twinges, comes to ground in his gums. Dull pain throbs around the lower molar and diminishes to nothing as *the problem* returns. He sticks a thumb into his mouth and touches the pain alive. Give me strength. Father, make me the killer I need to be. He reaches for the bottle, but his hand hovers like that of a toddler who remembers a burn. A coward's course. What makes the elephant charge his tusk?

He grins at the clearly remembered song and goes to the filmed window. Twelve floors down fuzzy headlights string the snow-banked length of Bloor for as far as his sharp grey eyes can see; brake lights wink like florescent rubies alongside a necklace of pearls. City ain't so bad, at night. Though in daylight only the sluggish filth stands out, the exhaust like smoke from some ceaselessly smouldering chemical dump. An ambulance swings from the line of cars and whoops down the centre of the street like a demented crane.

"Our own place outside the city!" But she can't hear. She's way out there, widening even further with her unconcern for punctuality the distance between us. How very poetic. *Fuck her.* Let her go! To hell and worse. To Limbo.

But why is it he feels no hatred for the quack? His father would have choked a . . . a cuckolder. Yes, that's the old word. With his bare hands! But *he* feels nothing. In fact, he has to resist the persistent twinges of . . . gratitude? Should he have raged, cocked fists and crowed when he got her home from parties where she'd openly flirted with Jim, flaunting their trust? *Trust?* She doesn't know the meaning of the word . . . the hooer! *There's* his father's voice. The ungrateful hooering cunt! No—wait . . . Fuck her anyway for an ungrateful cunting hooer!

Again he touches his tooth, and the pain's memory is there yet, a dulled throb, numbed distraction, like this city, or their endless falling-apart coming-together game. Her threats about his drinking, countered by his sneering at her sickeningly conventional wee-Cathy dreams of an emerald home in the ersatz countryside. I've seen the countryside! I grew up there, *remember?* It's shit! Endless thankless work and shit everywhere! But as the throbbing soon diminishes, so too does his passion. And like a practical Christmas gift intrudes the memory of his mother's story of Finn McCool and his tooth of knowledge, touched to tap communal fortunes, to see the unalterable future.

He is seven years old. His bum itches. There are worms in his poop. He pads upstairs and finds his mother sitting on the closed toilet. She doesn't know he's watching. He wishes he wasn't. Her face is to the window and she holds her apron crumpled in her white hands and she shakes her head and clucks her tongue forever before speaking: "What's to become of us?" She buries her face in the apron.

He slips downstairs and returns heavily.

"Is that you?" she calls.

"What're you doin'? My bum itches again."

"Just restin' a bit."

"On the toilet!"

She keeps her face averted as she passes him. He locks the door and sits on the closed toilet. In the sideyard his father kneels alongside his mother's garden and with uncharacteristic gentleness slides a square black stone along the edge of a spade. A perfect day. He doesn't want to stay inside forever. His oldest brother is eighteen. Pat, the youngest of seven, will be starting school next Fall.

That day he watched his mother closely, and she seemed a strange woman with a girl trapped inside her. That night, while his father was still in the barn, she told him the first story of Finn fishing for days to catch the magical trout.

"Say a prayer for all of us," she whispered closing the bedroom door, a catch in her voice.

And before he slept she was an old woman again.

He couldn't live alone! He can't envision himself in the sleeze bars on Yonge. He passes a tepid hand through the salted black hair drawing back from his forehead like . . . like his old man's, is all he can imagine. "Can't live with 'em, can't live without 'em," he sneers out the side of his mouth. His father's favourite line has become his *problem*. He wants his father's strength, just a touch to fire his flagging resolve.

To the ice bucket. Yes-yes, to the well! The frozen fish for the sacred tooth. The phone rings.

"Hello." Indifferently for her.

"Michael please don't hang up I've just gotta talk to you, is Catherine there?"

"No."

"Believe me Michael I'm so torn up about this that I couldn't stay in the office today. Catherine told me she told you, you must believe me it was all my fault."

"Of course it was your fault."

"Michael, you have just cause to feel wronged, but I'm not conditioned to alcohol myself. We were snowed-in by this freak storm and drinking because the furnace malfunctioned and . . ." He begins panting like a cried-out child.

The heat cut out? She'd not mentioned that. So careless had she forgotten some detail of deception? "Doctor—"

"Jim, please."

Is he whimpering? "Doctor Faubert, this has nothing more to do with you. Or do you enjoy this bit of emotional slumming? Is this a, uh, *growing experience?*"

"Pardon, Michael? I don't understand. Humour? . . . Michael, are you still on the line?"

"Prick."

"Michael, you have every right to feel wronged, as I believe I've already conceded. But surely you *of all people* can empathize with the fact that we were both intoxicated."

No surprise, she'd complained to her lover. "In vino veritas, shitbag."

"Michael, in view of the situation, I'm making an effort to overlook these anal epithets."

The bugger snickered.

"But we must, all three of us, get together tonight and work out what was, in all truthfulness, a very small misunderstanding."

"A *ménage à trois?* How groupy!"

"Michael, this could prove to be the most rewarding grow— *learning* experience of your married relationship. And your attitude won't—"

"Listen, this *relationship—my marriage—* was a leaky raft long before you boarder her. You're just the boring prick that's finally sunk her." He hangs up. At least while his wit remained there was hope for wisdom.

But why that twit with his *relationships, communicating,* and *experiences?* Should *he* have babbled like that to her? Would it have made a difference if she'd made it with someone he admires? Michael tries to think of someone he admires. Maybe John Lennon, before he married that Yoko.

Though she *was* drunk after two gins. What if the head-shrinker was telling his version of the truth? But why confuse the simple truth? Some things are not relative! Cannot be compromised! Are not negotiable! Her getting drunk only made it worse—using his favourite excuse to betray him! Whatever, they were finished. And really, who gives a living shit.

He again speaks aloud to mock her, though his assumed falsetto is as far from her voice as is his own: "He didn't achieve penetration, Mikey. Honestly!" *Achieve?* Good God, what're we talking about? Some junior pseudo-business? "He couldn't maintain an erection. We just passed out by the fire." *What?* Couldn't maintain an erection? Tch. And you primed. For the loving Jesus! *That's* your explanation-*cum* (if you'll pardon the expression)-apology? "Mich—" What, you didn't wire each other and monitor glandular secretions? Missed your chance, baby, could've been a new team of masturbating Johnsons. (Yes, his wit is intact; that's something anyway; and that "baby" was a nice touch.) "We were *drunk*, Michael. You know. Nothing happened!"

But if nothing, what then had she confessed to?

Michael sings: "I wanna caveman, I wanna brave man, Mikey show me that you care, really care for me-ee." He looks about the cramped living room. "We share," he whines. Everything, that is, but my booze bill. Though she'd needed a few stiff gins before spilling it. *In vino veritas.*

He turns to the liquor cabinet, fills his glass and drinks it straight off. He refills. They'd talked often of *space*, personal space, head space, space to grow in, *space* more than money or children. Suffering Jesus, what were we? Fucking astronauts? Well, she could have the whole empty universe! With her ugly hooked nose like a beak in his heart, he'd always hated it, but what's he thinking? Who cares who cares who cares. If the tooth won't work, his favourite poem will do the trick, but first a libation, to what was, what is, and whatever will be will be, "Que sera sera . . ."

In the fresh belly warmth, she seems a receding speck, an insignificant flutter. He draws a bead on his old highschool poetry anthology and with the singlemindedness of the denying drunkard walks a swaying line to the book case. He opens the book, blinks strenuously, and intones in a voice he imagines to be his fathers; but his slurring props his voice ludicrously on the stage Irish, so in a voice more Barry Fitzgerald's than his father's he reads: "Turning and turning in the widening gyre, the falcon cannot hear the falconer; things fall apart . . ."

One thought fascinates Cathy as she stands in the foyer flapping the snow from her arms like an unbalanced crow. How had she let Jim go so far, drunk or not, a twit like him? The disgusting business had started professionally enough. But why hadn't she recognized the nervous boy's ploy: a massage to help her relax, she was carrying too heavy a case load, wine for warmth. And just like a virgin highschool boy soddened by lemon gin, Jim had cried his limp apologies as she'd unwound into unconsciousness. "The penetrating psychologist's realm," she whispers and smiles at her faint smiling ghost in the glass door. Oh well, at least I've kept my sense of humour. That's something.

She'd awakened that morning on a hard floor, awakened to distant snoring and the chilling white of the fireplace. Three burnt, yet intact logs rested at eye level in a delicate tension, like three tubes of chalk, a geometry of delayed dust, *memento mori*. She'd yawned and shaken her head: meaningless, really.

But images from the previous night impinged, so she shut her eyes. Chalk . . . that's all . . . She let herself sink, the dream of the warm schoolroom back in Port Lambton like a friendly ghost in the cold room. Sister Patricia clomps down the echoing hall to assign the boys to men's jobs: "It's only early October, boys and girls, but it looks like we're in for a long cold Winter. So we may as well get some things straight. You shovel the walk. You clean the boards. You clap the brushes, *outside*." The girls, always her pets, are sent to the storeroom to luxuriate in the warm sweet odour of old and new books. So simple . . . She had blinked strenuously. Where the hell was she?

"Michael!"

"Zounds!"

Keep it together, she'd kept cautioning herself as she zipped and buttoned, and at the same time she'd had to fight an inappropriate urge to laugh at Jim's old-fashioned curse. Michael . . . not back from Sarnia till Friday, tomorrow, thank God. Still after the Dome account. Or is today tomorrow?

"Of course I'm going to tell him," she'd snapped at the bloodshot eyes that found yet more tears. "We're quite open."

At first he'd looked endearingly like a little boy who'd awakened from a nap in her lap, his dark hair falling from his long narrow head aslant his forehead and brown eyes like two pools of milk chocolate, his pale, hairless chest heaving, his buckle still undone. Then everyone's stage mother, walking in circles and wringing his hands, pleading with her to take a cab and not to tell Michael.

As she'd high-stepped through the fallen and falling snow, she was relieved at the absence of useless guilt feelings. She smirked, once again bemused at the way men could change so suddenly into boys. She had stopped smirking at the thought of Michael like a child, always telling her his mother's stupid stories about Cool-somebody. As though she should do the same! Men never grow up. He's totally irresponsible.

She had caught her hand to her heart that morning when he appeared lounging on the made bed, his head pressed against the headboard at an angle that betrayed his posed comfort, a bottle of the expensive Jameson's wedged between his thighs. His washed-out eyes, sleepy, though not yet drunk, had begged her to lie. Come back, they'd pleaded from a great distance below her. Head of her childless family, and her temperature up these past three days. She would be thirty-eight next month. That would have been his first bottle in months. Unless he'd been drinking when away. She wouldn't put it past him. Many times she'd threatened divorce over his boozing. And then she'd had to resist the twinges of disappointment when he'd quit. Drunk, he'd been passionately selfish, a different person, then eager to please when hungover. Sober, he'd grown indifferent, had let her go. And she'd gone.

At the Brass Rail Eddie Taylor agrees with Cathy. No doubt the ol' Mick is sterile, if not latently queer. But how on earth has Cathy managed to keep her figure? "No kiddin'? That much in six months?" He toasts her resolve with his light beer; she salutes the bar mirror with her gin fizz. In the mirror two policemen rush four boys towards the back door; a scuffle is heard, glass breaks, but Cathy doesn't look.

"Shit—excuse me," says Eddie and burps. "But, uh, like you're as sk—as slim as you were way back when at St. Pat's. Good ol' Sarnia. Here's to the Chemical Valley," he again toasts. "Long may she stink." He throws back his drink and slips off his stool. He reclaims his position.

When Gary Withers bumps into Michael at the Colony, he calls him Mikey and likes him again for the way he acts his old self. Michael laughs like old times back in Sarnia at Gary's extended jokes about Mr. and Mrs. Front Porch. In Mingles Gary ditches Michael, who is drunk and coming on to women in a way that had been embarrassing back in highschool. Michael even fails to get a laugh—let alone impress anyone—with the term of his terminal illness. The young women take him seriously, but don't appear to care.

Alone and fighting a premature hangover, Michael manages to make the acquaintance of the kind of woman Gary had warned him from, the "Classic Mingles": a seemingly well-preserved woman, freed from her first husband; a smoker of extra-mild cigarettes who is about to quit; a user of soft drugs who is thirsty for mineral water and meaningful conversation. "But that's not completely fair," even Gary had felt compelled to add. Michael's woman is alluringly dressed in some material that sparkles and shines, her hair sparkles too. He is enthralled by her forward and chippy conversation, and he thinks he is genuinely moved by the pathos of her excessive and chipped make-up. He tells her he is going to die soon and that he loves her. She stares at him blankly for a long while, then laughs: "I think I *do* know you after all." When she has consumed her way from water, through white wine and light beer, to straight scotch, she talks openly of the female orgasm. She impresses Michael to no end with the claim that she can orchestrate a simultaneous orgasm.

"G'won, tha's impossible!" And the beer trickles down his chin.

The closing hour come round at last, the four of them rise like one disjointed beast. They leave their last drinks untouched, the men anxious about driving and performance, the women about their figures and bladders. All work up a passionate intensity as they slouch into the lighted night from their bars. The sidewalks are windswept with a winter's accumulation of sand. It stings the women's legs and whips the faces of the men who must keep heads up. Two are relieved that they've scored decently for a change; two wonder fleetingly what has become of their convictions.

Potlatch

I identified my parents' bodies. It was like looking at especially lurid photographs in one of those *True Detective* magazines. My mother wore the pink nightdress my wife and I had presented her on her seventieth birthday. (Apparently she'd not struggled, or she'd been surprised, or for some weird reason her murderers had composed her.) My father wore his once-white boxer shorts. (He considered jockey shorts a contributing factor in the effeminization of Western Man.) Father and Mother, they lay propped against the headboard and facing the TV. The TV cable strung them together like two bloody shrunken heads. They had been strangled and shot through the ears. Sound seeped into the picture like vague hushed warnings in a nightmare. Ironically, the TV played *Three's Company;* it had been a favourite of my father's, who liked the lead actor because he was the son of Tex Ritter, the one-time American singing cowboy.

The three de Polaire brothers were arrested immediately. Ballistics evidence and the brothers' remorseless dispositions sent them to prison for life, though "life" is not to be taken literally. The court reporter for the *Sarnia Spectator* calculated "twelve years tops." Front page news for three days, a horror story of horrible ironies, as follows.

My father, a tobacco farmer, had held a nominal position
with the Ministry of Transportation and Communications. For
forty years the provincial government had paid him one hundred
dollars a month for doing nothing, or next to it; a few times he
stood accessory to ribbon-cuttings opening highways. In his last
official act he pulled the switch that provided the Chippewa
Reserve with cable TV, ten years after cable had reached the
greater distance to his farm. In the newspaper picture of his final
civic ceremony, the dots and gaps that compose his face emanate
an unmistakable smoke signal of distress. But otherwise he did
nothing. And then one day he received a communiqué ordering
him to investigate the commercial operation of a satellite dish on
the Chippewa Reserve.

The de Polaires owned the dish. Everyone knew that. Many
Sarnians had paid the brothers either money or booze to watch
current movies and sporting events. My father himself had forked
over two bucks to watch the Holmes-Cooney fight, that latest
dispatching of a Great White Hope ("Cooney, no less," as my
father had drunkenly regretted on his return from the Reserve.)
The illegal satellite concession had made the terrifying de Polaires
more civilized, or at least less violent. They no longer terrorized
Sarnia's seedy downtown bars; instead they moved from table to
table soliciting customers, accepting free drafts and handing out
joints of home-grown grass—a kind of inter-racial potlatch.
Chamois de Polaire, six foot and a solid two hundred pounds, with
a shaggy head bulky as a buffalo's in which only the beady eyes
moved, Chamois de Polaire was rumored to be baring in tolerance
for once his broken yellow teeth like frozen husky piss—grinning
at white men! (Though, judging from their surname, the de
Polaires must have had some French blood coursing through their
vengeful veins.) Mad Dog and Arthur de Polaire were reported to
have cavorted on stage at the St. Clair Hotel and taught the Black
stripper, "Lady Dye," an obscene rain dance.

It could only have been guilt over the unearned stipend that
spurred my father out to the Reserve upwind from Sarnia's

stinking Chemical Valley to order the de Polaire's to cease and desist their piracy of the popular (American) culture.

Chamois brazenly told the tale in court, after being cited twice for contempt: the first for spitting when asked to take what he called the "white-ass oath"; the second for snarling at the cavalier Assistant Crown Prosecutor and asking if he had any daughters. (Chamois kissed the air in a sort of obscene mock-romantic manner, then mimed snaking his penis like a garden hose; Mad Dog and Arthur whooped.) On Dad's first visit the de Polaires got him drunk, and together they watched a pirated World Cup soccer match between England and Argentina. Hungover the next day my father returned and was threatened with having his balls shot off. (Chamois claimed that before reissuing the order Dad had leaned in the doorway for an hour and watched the last half of the movie *Missing*.) Three days later Dad showed up at the brothers' with four Sarnia policemen, two Ontario Provincial policemen, and a plainclothes R.C.M.P. Dad personally (and no doubt apologetically) began dismantling the satellite dish. It was the O.P.P. seargeant who took a sledge hammer and smashed it up, glaring challengingly at the raging and gun-wielding brothers as if to say, 'Top that!' It was the Mountie who tightened the handcuffs.

Two weeks later the brothers were released from the county jail, mostly because Dad had loudly refused to testify against them. Two days afterwards my parents were murdered.

Two months later Marge, my wife, insisted that I take a week's vacation alone up at her parents' cottage near Midland. At the front door she slipped an envelope into the inside pocket of my white summer suit. She held my lapels till I promised to visit the Jesuit martyrs' shrine and have a Mass said for the repose of my parents' souls. A devout Catholic she spoke without any inkling of irony. Our two children hung on her thighs and grinned shyly up at me. Mary blinked slowly, as though anxious about my return from some dangerous hunt. Duncan stared strangely as if expecting some violent outburst from *me*. Since the incident I'd been moving automatically through a mechanized world, my neck like a turret, my eyes like laser-guided guns. The whole business felt like some story I'd read and confused with the sort of nightmare that feels real for hours after awakening.

But off I drove. Mindless driving for hours. Feeling more like an aging scout on his last field trip than a great white hunter. I was tempted briefly to detour at Orillia and visit the humourist Stephen Leacock's summer home at Old Brewery Bay. I've always wanted to learn more about that odd mixture of a man, who wrote so brilliantly when he took the time. But the time didn't feel right for his bewildering ambivalence and difficult wit.

The last hundred metres of road to my in-laws' cottage is unpaved, and the cottage too, set high on a bluff and facing the bay, is still well hidden by pine trees. I parked at the back and walked wearily to the drop. Supposedly I was near where Huron Indians had watched for the canoes of their natural enemies, the marauding Iroquois. But the vista of Georgian Bay made me feel shrunken to one drop of frozen blood, and dead tired, a bone-weariness like nothing I'd ever suffered. I stared blankly at the water as though engaged in some contest of expressionlessness, till I realized with a start that I was nodding off towards the water.

I determined to stay but the one night, rise early, commission the Mass, then head home. I flopped onto the musty mattress at six, not bothering with the sheets Marge had provided. I drifted off to the sounds of wind and water, a few hydro wires buzzing like tree toads . . . no phone . . . that was relief . . .

It was a sleep filled with vague whispered warnings and mindless violence. My only relief was the rhythmic pumping of my legs as I ran from scene to scene: a boxing ring, my old father confronting Redcoats and Indians wielding machetes and wearing headphones, Dad's ears are cut off, he fights on as I run on . . . my mother's face in one of those old paperweight snowstorms, the fluid turns to blood, the snow is nuclear fallout, her face would fill a drive-in screen, her eyes terrified, her mouth working silently what I know to be my name, she cups an ear, and I run on, plod drowsily and uncaringly through a mined poppy field, explosions underfoot and whizzing shrapnel, which scores but doesn't hurt. . . And I awoke laughing and singing softly to myself, "We're out of the woods, we're out of the dark, we're out of the night . . ."

It was six in the morning. I was overcome by guilt. It seemed I'd made cheap horror of my parents' murders. Even nightmares should not be allowed such licence.

I searched vainly for a meaningful story in my nightmare. I tried to sink back into a half-sleep, knowing that in a semi-conscious state I'd often before woven a narrative thread through disjointed dreaming, and felt better for the effort. But I failed to· drift off, perhaps because I felt that making sense would be doing violence to the spirit of my dream.

I got up and headed straight for the unpacked car. I would grab something at one of the many fast-food outlets that line the main drag to the fort and shrine. Or I would fast. Though I wouldn't take Communion.

Early though it was, the faithful trudged upwards to the shrine: a blind Black boy with a white cane lagged behind his back-glancing parents and impatient younger sister; an inappropriately laughing man snapped pictures of a woman who sat coyly on the guardrail and talked with her hands; two nuns on four canes jabbered loudly. Just beyond the traditional habits of the nuns, my progress all but stalled.

I rolled slowly upwards behind a Volkswagen van. When I saw daylight I shot from the processional and drove to the last empty section by the back of the church. Only when I stood in the cool breeze from the bay did I realize how much I was sweating. But the ignorant faithful have always affected me so. I was tempted to walk in the empty flower gardens that fell away to the left and the lake. But, as before with the impulse to visit Orillia, the time wasn't right. I was determined to make a quick business of my mission. I turned toward the church—

"Hey, buddy."

A boy stood by the trunk of a stunted maple tree. He too was short and slight, with straight black hair to his shoulders. He was an Indian.

"Wanna buy some weed?"

"No thanks."

"Scared?" He seemed always to be sneering,

"No," I grinned sheepishly, "it's just that . . ." But I decided to hell with him and apologies. I turned, figuring that if worse came to worst—if he had thinner friends behind the pines—I could always scream and run for the church; if only worse, he looked a size this great white hope could handle.

"How 'bout some coke then? Enjoy the show more after a snort."

I turned back: "I said *no*. Don't you understand plain English?"

"Chickenshit," he sneered more deeply and looked nervously about. "White-ass."

"Right. And just where would a little brave like you get uncut cocaine up here?"

"Up my fucking asshole," though he cupped his crotch.

"Then eat this shit, wagonburner," and I drew a sawed-off shotgun from inside my jacket and blew him into the happy hunting grounds.

That didn't really happen. I said, "Then eat shit, wagonburner," and took a step towards him. He ran. I slowly filled my lungs. You take what you can get. I went looking for a priest.

Temporary signs in wheel rims lined the walk between the back of the church and a one-storey white building. The first and largest sign announced a "Special Requests Mass" at seven that morning, which explained the pilgrimage of afflicted. I decided to try for a ranking cleric in what the last sign pointed toward: "This Way," above a red arrow indicating the lakeside of the church, and below the arrow, "Photo Arbor Of Martyrs."

The martyrs of the arbor stood along cement walks. I came up short at a life-sized replica designated "Frère Brébeuf," and I thought that the good Brother had suffered further some vandal's violence: his head was missing. Then I noticed the pillory notch where the subject of the "photo" was to place his faithful pate. (I see already that the business above about the shooting was a mistake. Because of it no one will believe me here. Yet you can travel to Midland and the Martyrs' Shrine and check out The Photo Arbor Of Martyrs for yourself.)

I continued up the hill, not a priest in sight to set me free and send me home. I encountered the headless Massé, Jogues, and the Lalemant frères with an arm around each other's vacant shoulders like buddies at a union picnic. At the very summit stood a headless, displaced St. Francis of Assisi! A decapitated cardboard bear languished at his sandaled feet; a pigeon with inhumanly tiny head perched on his flat forefinger, waiting to confirm murmuringly the serenity of whatever placid mug occupied the pillory notch. Why St. Francis? Who knows. The administrators of that travesty may have felt that his upbeat relationship with the furry kindred nicely offset the downer of the Martyrs.

I looked carefully all around to confirm that the arbor was absolutely empty. I stood behind kind St. Francis, fit my head to his shoulders, and laughed aloud.

"Would you like to be immortalized?"

I retracted my head and turned to find an old priest in open-collared black cassock. I quickly assumed that he'd meant would I like to have my picture taken: "Uh, I don't think I could afford it, Father. Just browsing."

He chuckled as though to himself. "We do have a Polaroid in the, uh, office." He cocked his white-haired head at the low white building, then squinted wryly.

"Only if you have a cut-out of the Grand Inquisitor lighting up Jean D'Arc's life."

He snorted slightly as he struck a mock *mea culpa:* "Ah irony, soul of humour."

He glanced toward the church, winked familiarly at me, then drew a slightly trembling, liver-spotted hand down his cheeks: "Pays the bills, you know." With practiced unselfconsciousness he clasped his left wrist behind his back and assumed a delcamatory tone: "Never denigrate the almighty . . . uh, dollar!" He winked again and walked on.

I laughed in genuine appreciation and called, "Father?"

He paused but didn't turn back.

"Has anyone ever told you you're the spit-and-image of Stephen Leacock?"

He faced me, a grin successfully fighting the frown that failed to draw his pious look. "Here about? Manys the time. The image, anyway." He gestured at my St. Francis' body: "Only the flesh, Brother Jackass, eh?" He swept his arm in the general direction of the church: "In fact, when I fought against *this* testimony to faith and humility, good Monsignor Garret called me the *brazen* image of old Leaky Steamcock." He smirked and headed down the hill.

"Father," I called, "do you believe then in reincarnation?" I snickered loudly like a self-congratulatory fool.

He paused and stared at his feet, his back to me: "A joke's a joke, my son, but I'm having difficulty convincing *them* of the incarnation." He proceeded downward.

But what was I thinking? "Father, can I, uh, commission you to say a Mass for the repose of my parents' souls?"

"Inside," he waved dismissively at the church. Young Father Chuck. He handles all *those* commissions." He moved gingerly along the declination.

"They were murdered two months ago by Indians," I said in my normal voice.

"You're not to be trusted, son," he shouted. "But God bless you anyway. You look like you need it." With two fingers he waved a confused sign of the cross over his head, then vanished as suddenly as he'd appeared.

"Thank you . . . *sir*," I shouted back. To hell with him. My father was dead.

I looked about the arbor of martyrs, then across at the church. My head was level with the base of its especially busy stained-glass windows. What's a little hypocrisy compared to *this*? Have the Mass said.

The church was packed, with the afflicted occupying the front pews. A young priest talked into a hand-held microphone. Below permed blond curls he sported pink plastic glasses and a black T-shirt with a flecked logo I couldn't make out. Father Chuck. I could see he was an entertainer: the congregation was grinning smugly as if to say as one body, "We can dig it." He paced the elevated near-side of the Communion rail, flipping the cord of his mike behind him like a pro. He was in short the sort of priest I would dismiss as a caricature poorly executed if I met him in a movie or novel. Yet Father Chuck was oblivious to the figure he cut.

"I kid you not," he said, holding up his hand to quell the almost-dead-anyway tittering. "But to get serious for a moment. . . ."

He briefly related the history of the shrine and its relics, and vouched for the veracity of the crutches, folded wheelchairs and prosthetic devices stacked higher than the altar. He made no promises, though. He looked only at the clock above our heads at the back.

There was a commotion up front. A knot of people inched towards the side exit as though chained ankle to ankle. The congregation shifted and buzzed.

The middle-aged man standing beside me caught my eye and winked inappropriately, nervously. He was dressed in the flat-green outfit of construction workers, was full-faced, broad-nosed, and bald but for a thin, back-combed mousy fringe on the last third of his dome. His swollen nose and pinkishly tinged scalp argued that he'd come for *the* cure. "It's like this *every* day of the summer," he whispered breathily. "It's the excitement of expectations, too much for *some*."

"What a fucking joke," I whispered.

He frowned and moved in front of me. "You'll have to excuse me, I'd better go see if I can help the poor soul." He touched my shoulder: "And it's not a joke, son. It's the only way nowadays the Church can *communicate* with her children."

He made his way through the jam at the back, headed, I supposed, to his glove compartment for a swig. I wished I'd kept my silence. I wished I was a drinker.

A disconcerted Father Chuck flipped his cord like a failed
attempt to snake a skipping rope. "It's *only* the heat and excite-
ment," he drawled, affecting boredom. He snapped his cord like
a bullwhip and snagged it on the wound-iron leg of a candle
display. He tugged at the cord as he hollered, "There were these
two Hispanic nuns wanted to come here in August with parkas.
The first said, 'Si-si, Seester, zee Canadas are muchos frigidaire!'"
He jerked his cord and moved his lips. Nothing.

The congregation caught its breath and looked to the ceiling,
and in that instant of hallowed silence a boy wailed, "I wanna see
real Indians *now!* "

Someone carrying the body shouted, "Call an ambulance,
please! She's swallowed her tongue!"

Over the ensuing shouts and few screams Father Chuck
bellowed,"Better hers than mine, eh!" Then despairing of laughter
he wailed,"Ned! Where the hell are ya Ned!" and looked directly
at me.

"Here Chuck!" someone shouted from the right aisle. A
raised arm like a periscope cleaved through the sea of humanity
streaming for the exits.

"We've lost our juice, Ned!" shouted Father Chuck.

The periscopic arm rose as Ned stepped up onto the Com-
munion kneeler. He was the Man who'd stood beside me. He
conferred with Father Chuck then exited stage left.

Father Chuck hollered clearly over the turmoil: "It's just, a
minor, communications, problem. *Really!* Ned'll have us wired
right in a jiff. The unfortunate person is being seen to *in our own
infirmary.* Please, just sit tight. Those who leave are going to miss
out on the, uh . . . the *special* I was just about to announce." —A
freeze-frame— "That's more like it." He patted the air as though
clumsily playing an organ.

Ned the Super returned with an imposing stepladder bang-
ing against his thigh. He erected it like a steeple and spread its legs.
He took the disengaged end of the cord and climbed to a box set
high on the pillar adjacent to the pulpit.

He was down in a minute, the microphone in his hand: "Testing, testing, ah . . . one-two-buckle-my-shoe." The congregation guffawed and waved him off. "You're back in business, Father C," Ned grinned broadly.

The congregation laughed, someone shouted, "More! More!"

A tightlipped Father Chuck hurried to his calling, head shaking after the efficient Ned as if he were praying silently for a pratfall. "Well then, where was I?" he mused.

"The *special*," some matron shouted. Loud relieved laughter.

Exiting through the vestibule I heard the priest begin, *Introibo*: "Yes, well, just to show you I'm a man of my word, I'm going to have ol' chromedome bring over a carton of holy oil vials, and everyone who stayed can have *two* for the price of one!"

White light and searing heat—the shoved church doors opened into a furnace. Whatever vestige of hope for consolation I'd childishly clung to was whited-out like a typographical error, burned away like a stuck movie frame, eliminated like background noise. Only in bad romances and simple movies do characters "come to terms," by means of memory usually, the palliative past, by a kind of memory-mining for idiot's nuggets with which to stud the sordid present. A charmingly valiant pursuit, though futile. And anyway, it can't be mine.

Mine is a time of subsuming violence to body and spirit. The real priests strain to entertain, the priests of art are playfully pained entertainers. The true high priest is leering Violence, his distorting form lording it over us all. Father, what's to be made of such insistent, stinking reality? Transmute it? But how? A new alembic for the old narratrickery? Do violence to violence? . . . Father, take that cup away. I'd rather sit for eternity at a stiff Underwood writing ironized Westerns, with a jockstrap over my nose.

The traitorous tourists tripped about the knolls of the Photo Arbor of Martyrs, posing then excitedly changing places like self-important nits on some tired animal's hide. "They're giving away free vials of holy oil!" a boy shouted behind me. And the would-be martyrs leapt from the arbor like lice from a burning bear. *Vile's* the word. Those in the rear (gentle St. Francis?) looked ready to murder for their unearned splashes, their connection to the Sacred . . . as the de Polaire brothers had murdered my parents for killing their satellite concession, their connection to the white man's sacrosanct airwaves and affluence. . . . *My*, isn't *that* ironic, I spat, but wind caught the gob and looped it back on my chin.

Though I couldn't have imagined the possibility (my failing), I felt wearier than when I'd arrived at the cottage. I stopped squinting, closed my eyes and patted my breast pocket: twenty bucks. I could buy a few books with that.

I lie upside-down on my made bed, feet crossed on the pillow, fingers knitted behind my head, eyes squinting at the white ceiling whose reassuringly random plaster pimples are being painstakingly defined by daybreak. It is my third day at the Holiday Inn on the fringes of Orillia. A call to my wife is overdue. But what in hell does she expect me to report? . . . So downside-up on my made bed lie I.

"Oh sweetheart, it was an inspired idea! A miracle of female intuition and imagination! Now don't talk, just listen. And I apologize beforehand if I gross you out. *And* for the delay. But this is no time for sensitivity.

"Honey, I'll admit up front that for the first couple of days I felt jumpy and just plain pissed-off at creation. After the memorial Mass for Dad and Mom, I walked over to Fort Huronia. The Mass hadn't helped much, and I'd decided to head straight home after visiting the fort. But a weird thing happened at the fort.

"I let the tour group I was in move on to the rustic chapel without me. As I stood alone by the palisade along the canoe canal, I suddenly got off on the windowpane acid I'd bought from this Indian kid outside the fort. *Buzzzzzz*, a rush from head to toe like an eagle feather pulled the length of my esophagus. I closed my eyes, my soul vibrated, my spirit soared.

"When I opened my eyes I was standing in the midst of kneeling black-robed frères and half-naked Hurons. Out of the violet-ringing air Iroquois came tearing over the pointed posts of the barricade, others appeared to arise from the very waters of the great brown canal, still others full-blown from the ribbed surface of the palisades. The Hurons leapt and ran screaming. Their heads were whacked wide, battered brains oozed like jellied cauliflower. Frenzied Iroquois dipped fingers in steaming cortex and hurriedly crossed themselves in mock-piety. The good brothers ignored (as best they could, given the circumstances) the commotion and challenging glares of the Iroquois—Top that!—and remained kneeling in skittish supplication as their charges—the braves, squaws and infants (papoose in *tikanagan*)—were massacred, dismembered and flung hither and thither and yon. An ancient brave and squaw were cuffed about the ears and dismembered at my feet. I felt nothing.

"The patient frères were dragged off one by one, tied to makeshift totems, tortured, taunted, terminated. Brébeuf appeared without heart for the proceedings. One of the smaller Iroquois, a filthy little brave, stuck his face up close to Ragueneau's (this time no one escaped) and chanted a bad sarcastic poem about Brébeuf. Egged on by his confréres he accompanied his verse with sexually degrading gestures. Transcribed phonetically, his name was On-wel-tar-get, which, translated liberally, is Iroquois for 'I am were I am, this very spot here, the ground on which I stand at present, right here, now.' When he finished he said, 'We are doing you heap big favour, Black Robe. I mean, ugh, like by martyring you. Is that not the supreme irony, eh?' He then forced the gentle frère to view some negatives of obscenely sacrilegious photographs, or so he (the native) must have thought them.

"Ragueneau broke down and prayed to Sainte Ignatious for the release of death. As that brought no cessation to his suffering, he begged his tormentors for same. But they were not yet disposed to comply. So I brazenly entered the scuffle.

"With my hand held high I recited a bad satiric-ironic poem which began, 'My children were murdered by Indians.' The

Iroquois high-tailed it. In their haste some slipped atop the palisades and wriggled there impaled on the points: a few with the points up through their chins and out their eyes, others with the points under their breastbones and lancing them like ill-spitted pigs, a number with the points pinning them asshole-wise like the specimens of a sadistic entomologist. And it was over. This white man had done enough.

"I sauntered off feeling light as air. The only sensation to which I can compare my euphoria is the way I felt walking down the aisle after my First Confession.

"Honey, it was inspired magic, white magic, the best idea in the *whole* world! It worked like fighting fire with fire, violence purging violence—a sort of psychic potlatch! Now I know the true meaning of catharsis—metacatharsis!

"Honey, did you expect this would happen? Did you? Is this what you expected? Don't lie just to please me! *Is this what you wanted to happen?*"

I opened my eyes. Only four days to go. Who knows, I might even be able to sleep now. I followed my strobing arm through the unreal light of dawn, switched on the bedside light, and picked from the night table my new coming-unglued copy of *Sunshine Sketches of a Little Town*. I began again: "I don't know whether you know Mariposa. If not, it is of no consequence, for if you know Canada at all . . ."

So much better than "I identified my parents' bodies." And the train to Mariposa! Ah that little town in the sunshine that once we knew. *En voiture!* . . . It was either that or the letter opener I'd purchased at the Old Brewery Bay souvenir trailer and inadvertently honed to stiletto on the iron runners of my made bed. . . . But I have no letters to open. My quarrel is not with the alphabet.

The Go-Away Game

I

Diane squints at the new crossroads from the one narrow window of the empty classroom. It is a meeting of three roads, one of which runs haphazardly past Hank's farm to her own home three-quarters of a mile from the new school. Another road, familiar, leads straight into the city three miles away. And the new road, still black and soft, twists around Hank's property to the new suburb of half-finished houses.

She tightens her compressed lips and shakes her head at the city kids boarding their busses. The clowning boys jostle and bump each other into the girls, who drop jaws and swat in mimed outrage. And for once Diane is grateful that the room is partially soundproofed, knowing how she would simply loathe those helpless girlish shrieks.

The yellow and black busses continue inching into position like massive bees sluggish to evacuate eggs from a burning hive. A few kids walk past Diane's window on their way to the new suburb, oblivious to the queenly scorn she is failing to maintain, let alone master. And the go-away game, it too is failing her.

That throbbing again in her temples, the sharp pains behind her eyes. She closes her eyes and concentrates all her waning powers on the go-away game, daring the pain and failure. Her head vibrates from the effort. When she opens her eyes a slit she can't see the new road. She smiles with teasing malevolence at this return of her powers. But the black road shimmers back, vanishes, then emerges mesmerizingly like the face of a dear enemy in a developing photograph. Her thumbnail splits on the new window putty. Now she'll have to cut them all, "de-claw" herself, as her mother says.

At least the window still provides a reassuring view of Hank's old place across the new road. A reassuring view: Hanks' house like a country carnival's idea of horror, his sagging barn with her father's useless red elevator hanging like a panting hound's tongue from the worthless loft. *Worthless* because Clefton Developers had bought off the buyers to ensure that Hank's harvest would be left for rats. Diane hates Clefton, and not only because she loves Hank.

Dumb old farmer, she thinks, shaking her head then pressing her cheek against the window. To the right the tar-papered houses, as monotonous now as they would be when completed, worry her further. But she will not force the go-away game again, no, let it gather her hidden strength. She merely stares disgustedly at the newly paved road disappearing into the black boxes, a road flanked by raw ditches whose mounds sprout dusty fleabane, browning crabgrass and broken burdock, here and there the filthied white of a drooping Queen Anne's Lace. The long Thanksgiving weekend is already over, another promised completion date missed. It looks to Diane as if they're never going to finish the new suburb, though her new neighbours—the luckier ones—complain little about having to live in a skeletal community.

She brings the split thumbnail to her mouth. Already the novelty of the new school has worn thin, as prematurely threadbare as the bleached and patched bib overalls the city boys now like to wear. *Nor*, she says to herself, is it exciting any longer taking assembly with the so-called Seniors. It's the same now with the Ball as it was last June when no one asked her to the Prom. And even if she is sexy in a way that her mother calls wholesome (though her mother says "attractive"), it doesn't balance things. It doesn't look like anything's *ever* going to change.

The only big difference so far is that Hank has surprised everyone and harvested his fields practically single-handedly. There were rumours that Clefton paid some of the remaining farmers not to help him. They want his land that badly. But Diane's father got the loan of Fleming's combine and helped out on weekends. Still, that's not really the only *big* difference, it's the only difference, romantically speaking.

The goofy "Senior" boys in Diane's class went after the new crop of grade-nine girls like tongue-drooling mutts. They were *supposed* to fall over each other trying to be the first to ask her to Immaculate Conception's gala Harvest Moon Ball tonight. *Why* she had let herself dream they would, praying to St. Jude all summer long like some silly immature grade-niner . . . Well, it's beyond her. She's too aloof. She should know by now that beautiful legs and a sexy figure aren't enough to get immature boys to approach *her* for a date. She must remain aloof, assume a queenly bearing. It takes goofy boys time to realize that they're supposed to want what they think they can't get. Or so her mother says. "Yes, mother," she whispers to her transparent reflection on the window, "they're simply *paralyzed* with respect for me." Beyond her pale image the black road shimmers briefly.

The nerd girls didn't even nominate me for the decorating committee, that last refuge of the wallflower. And rightly so, when you come right down to it. Could a woman who doesn't wear mascara paint an enticing poster? Does a T-shirt where a bra is needed suggest a sense of decorum? . . . And now, to tip the scales against me, I'm losing my power at the go-away game.

I should be more like Hank, she determines, sucking on her thumb. I should stick to my guns and not even hope for things I don't really want, or need. If I could keep just one promise to myself the way he's stood up to Clefton and hung on to his farm . . . Well, for one thing I *wouldn't* have been left standing by Pat Fletcher's locker today, cow-eyed and mooning like Hank's Selly when Pat took off after that flirt, Debbie Summers. It's bad enough that I stood there listening to Pat joke about Hank-the-hick-Burroughs (as he calls him), thinking like an absolute *goof* that his next breath was my invitation to the Ball. But to have to take Summers', "Hi Di, nice leotards. Oh Pat, after assembly some of us kids are going to The Golden Hind for coffee and toasted cinnamon rolls. Coming?" Well, I nearly died inside. And Fletcher takes off after that slut without so much as a see-ya-later. (Really, what good is it having shapely legs when you're the only sixteen-year-old woman left in the universe whose mother won't let her shave her legs and still makes her wear ankle socks over green woollen leotards?)

Oh, but I saw it coming, almost like I made it happen. I did. But who needs the whole yapping pack of them? They probably think that I'm as big a hick as Hank. . . . That's hard to think: "As big a hick as Hank as big a hick as Hank as big as hick a—"

Control yourself, Di dear. Don't want to be caught talking out loud to yourself. No-no. Like the time Summers and Laura LeClair caught me reciting my favourite poem and Summers said, "Get a load of little Anne Shirley." I *loathed* that *stupid* movie and that oh-so-cute hayseed girl. . . . Control yourself. You'd better get the eggs from Hank or Mom won't even let you go to the Ball with cousin Billy, the original hayseed. He's so easy to control he makes me want to puke.

"Pa-lee-ease, Mother, I simply *refuse* to go to Harvest Moon with Billy. It's so . . . so *très cliché*."

"Young lady, don't you use that tone of voice with me or you can just as soon stay home tonight and help put up the peaches." She softened: "You sound like a disgruntled Miss Piggy." She laughed.

"Mo-ther, this is not a joke."

So what? It is a joke. A new school. Big deal. My life's the same. I'll probably die an old maid, a scrawny old virgin like Miss Lucy in the cafeteria. . . . Was I talking out loud again? Oh, I'm a lunatic, a lunatic, a luna— Settle down, Di. Control yourself. You'd better sit out by the bike racks for a while and compose yourself or Hank'll take one look at you and think I'm—think *you're* just like all the other jumpy kids. City idiots. Hank says that people can't be doing much better in the city, judging by the coveralls their kids wear. Big dumb farmer, he thinks the patches cover real holes. City idiots. Why do they paste manure on the wall at a *Sarnia* wedding? . . . To keep the flies off the bride. I've heard that one, and I get it.

She leaves the empty classroom, goes outside and sits on the browning new sod by the freshly painted bicycle racks. Hoping to catch a glimpse of Hank before he spots her, she shades her eyes and searches his yard. But he's nowhere to be seen.

Her parents worry that Hank has been growing strange since Mrs. Burrough's death three years ago. Just that morning Diane saw her father give her mother a funny look when she reminded Diane to stop in at Hank's place for the eggs. And when her mother caught the look she twitched her nose and told Diane not to be wasting time there but to come straight on home to help peel and pit the peaches.

But what do they think Hank is? She lifts the corner of a grass mat. No roots, no wonder. What do they think *I* am? I'm not a child, though they still treat me like one, don't even let me drink coffee, stunts my growth. Shit, if I grow any taller I'll be able to stick the cocks on weather vanes! And Mom almost dies of embarrassment whenever I mention the bra, even though my breasts are already as big—bigger than hers. And firm. So to hell with them. Hank's the only person in the world who treats me like an equal, like an adult. I'll stay and talk to him for a long as I like.

She rolls from one cheek to the other and draws up her right knee to prop her chin. Her dress falls back, revealing legs that are long, strong, and shapely in their green woollen leotards. She doesn't think to straighten the dress, but concentrates instead on Hank's barn. He's probably in there, milking and spouting to himself about the end of the world. When he talks he refers to himself in the third person—a mannerism that drives Diane right up the wall—and always says "the world as we know it." As if there were another. Fat chance.

Besides, what Hanks says can't hurt me. I hardly even listen to what he's saying, like when he talks about not having been able to make a baby with Mrs. Burroughs. (God, if Mom and Dad knew even the half of it!) I mean, you'd have to have a dirty mind to think he was seriously suggesting something. I just like to stand there watching him work. I love the smell of the barn. For that space of time there's nothing else in the universe, no school, no Clefton, no me in a strange way. And when I do talk he listens, like when I tell him that I want to be an agriculturalist when I grow up. I know he listens because he always says something sweet, like "Stick to your guns." Or that I belong here and the other kids are trespassers on what used to be the McKenzie place. Or Judas' place, as Hank calls him.

He even lets me milk sometimes. I'd keep going just for that. After sitting through forty minutes of Butch Shehan's sex-ed class every Friday, it's sheer pleasure to put on Hank's old plaid shirt and milk for a spell. I never would have believed that I'd actually miss *chores*, and then Dad sold Feebee.

But what's Mom so up-tight about? I'm not dumb. I know she thinks that there's something sexual in it. But that's *so* puritanical, the ultimate cliché. I mean, I've been taking sex-ed from *Mizz* Shehan for three years now. I probably know more about contraceptives than Mom. . . . It's just that I've missed the farm, the barn and the milking—all the animals, even the stupid chores—since Dad sold our place to that fucking Clefton! Goddamned sonofafucking— Easy, ease off, Di dear.

Diane's father still owns the farmhouse and about ten surrounding acres. But just last week, with her bedroom door ajar, she'd overheard her parents discussing the sale of the remaining land, and the house. Her father said that Mr. Clefton was ready to pay handsomely for the remaining property. For fifty thousand he could have one of the new houses on what used to be the far forty— a special consideration—and what with all the money he'd been paid for the rest of the land he could retire to Florida and not have to work another day in his life, if he didn't want to. Her mother had jokingly corrected him, saying "*We*, dear." Though she'd never had to do that before. And then seriously she'd said that, yes, it was something to think about. But before she could give it any further thought, Diane had jumped out of bed and stomped into the living room. Trying to draw one good breath but only catching short ones, she'd lost her calculated advantage. She lost control and began screaming that she'd run away from home if they sold their home.

Her father stiffened against the back of his chair as though he'd been rammed in the chest. He stared at her for a long moment as if bewildered by some stranger's claim. But he set aside the dog-eared farmers magazine he'd never before had time to read and went to her. She flinched some because it was the first time he'd held her in a year or so. He called her "Baby" again and told her not to have a conniption fit, that it was just idle talk, that he would never sell their home. They both looked to Mrs. Archer and waited for her nod. She set aside the new *Consumer's* catalogue, came over and stroked Diane's hair. Diane felt like a little kid again but didn't care because it felt good and nobody was watching anyway. Then her father started laughing, her mother laughed, Diane laughed, and laughing they soon felt even more awkward than when embarrassed into laughter. Her mother tapped Diane's ass and packed her off to bed, teasingly threatening no new dress for the Ball if she didn't stop eavesdropping and go to sleep.

Even with the door closed she heard her father say, "What's got into your daughter lately?" And her mother whispered, "It's what's been coming out of her that worries me."

Still, she slept soundly that night, secure in the warmth that had come from seeing her father laugh again—the first time he'd really laughed since selling the farm and taking the job digging Clefton's ditches. It was the only night since school had started that she didn't have to make herself sleepy by masturbating even once. In the morning she realized this and sat up and yawned and stretched for a good while. She felt cleansed, no matter what her sex-ed teacher says about its being perfectly natural. It's not what Diane thinks of as natural.

And to think, he actually thought about selling our home too! . . . Well, I haven't seen Hank so he must be in the house. A funny picture, his farm, what Mr. Milner would call anachronistic. This ultra modern school with scarcely a window, only one long

narrow one for each classroom like in a dungeon. They claim that
no windows lengthens our attention spans, or as they say, it
increases our efficiency. And this ugly box borders Hank's corn-
field, not a hundred feet from his house, a house that doesn't even
have running water, or an indoor bathroom. But I suppose that if
there were windows, ninety percent of the kids would spend
ninety percent of their time continuing the jokes about Hank-the-
hick-Burroughs' leaning tower of Pisa barn, his wash-n-wear
overalls, and the plaid shirt that doubles as pyjamas and dinner
jacket. City idiots, moving out here to what they call the sticks. I
used to be bussed to the old Immaculate Conception in the city,
now Sarnia's struck out to here and most of the kids are bussed to
the new Immaculate Conception. Wee-ird. City idiots, where the
hell do they think their food comes from? Big machines in the back
of the A&P? City idiots.

Once, when I was standing by the fence talking to Hank,
Mike O'Reilly walked by and said, "Hey Hank, how're you *making
out* with your sheep?" And Hank said, "What? You blind, son?
You see any sheep?" Even I knew what that pig O'Reilly meant,
the goof. That was when mutton shot sky high, and Hank was
caught raising bacon. I've even seen Debbie Summers point down
to my place and say that the lightning rods were used to bring life
to the Archer's monster daughter—that she still wears leotards to
hide the scars where they sewed her shins to her knees! Then the
slutty streak of misery said that her old man owned a house like
ours before he got a job. I nearly died inside, standing there not
three yards behind them. But then Pat Fletcher said he'd bet I was
a good lay with those muscular thighs, that I had a pretty foxy bod
and that he wouldn't throw me out of bed for eating crackers. And
even though it was sort of forward of him, I felt a feather's tickle
in my stomach, just thinking about it. I mean, being a good egg and
all that and eating crackers in bed with Pat. So I didn't make a
scene, just snuck into school unnoticed. I thought about Pat the
next few times I did it to myself. But forget about that, Di dear. If
you don't go see Hank right now you won't have any time to talk
to him.

The road changes from asphalt to gravel when it crosses Hank's property line. The grass alongside grows tougher, the kind that either cuts noticeably when touched or secretly slices fish gills in fingers. Diane is careful not to step on the blades of grass that grow through the white dusty gravel. She has been ever since she cried inside when Mr. Milner recited the poem about the graveyard and the flowers that wasted away in deserts. Her favourite poem. Every black tar-papered house of the unfinished suburb already has a sick maple sapling tied to a bumpy iron pole in the front yard dirt. Hank believes that those houses won't weather fifteen years, which is fine by him because he figures the world as we know it isn't going to last that long anyway. He says you can worry the world for only so long before she rears up and lashes back. People worry that pollution threatens the human race, but Hank says that's a very limited point of view. Big nature, the real thing, not forests and flowers, doesn't care dungpiles about having no clean water or no ozone. It's all the same to her. Human beings or cockroaches, or just nothing. It's not like she plays favourites. Imagine being *that* aloof, *that* powerful?

Hank's fence is down along the front, though the gate is still standing and wired shut with a clothes hanger. Just a short walk from the school, from what Hank calls "the building of higher ignorance," and soon Diane feels quiet, calm as she steps daintily across the prone fence and into a barnyard alive with stealthy cats and rooting pigs and scratch-dancing chickens, a yard littered with the rusted teeth of upside-down harrows and spreaders raking the air, outhouses flat on their backs, a yard mined with mires of steaming piss and shit. In the school she moves ponderously, bumping into suddenly jutting desk corners, or her square-piled books spill into the hall like locker guts when *she* attempts to touch up her hair in the pink plastic mirror inside the door. But in Hank's yard she almost feels graceful, more at home than she has felt recently in her real home. She thinks of shit as manure again, doesn't mind the sight or smell, knowing full well that the kids at school would have been friendlier this year if she hadn't been seen leaving Hank's dungyard so often—if Pat hadn't looked down last week and seen shit and straw pasted to her shoes, then simply cringed and walked away. And they would have been friendlier, she'd be going to the Ball tonight with a real date. Not that she cares.

There are three of them, they're Black, and they're sisters. That's all Diane knows. She will have to listen closely for their name the next time the song, her current favourite, comes on the radio. The "Oinker Sisters" or something, but that's crazy. Only punkers would call themselves that. And there are no Black punkers. Anyway, she flicks her hip, taps her right hand on her thigh, and sings, more loudly than is safe, the lines she memorized the first time she picked them out: "I'm so excited, and I just can't hide it; I'm about to lose control, and I think I like it. . . ."

"Hank?" As usual the door's wide open to the world. "Hank?" He's probably out in the barn, but better to check inside first, just to make sure he isn't lying dead in front of the radio, as Mom always says we'll find Hank one day. If only I could be more like Hank. Speak with my own voice instead of that lunatic's words that come from I don't know where whenever I open my mouth around the other kids. Even when I'm alone lately. Hey, You up there? Since You made me such a klutz, do You think you could at least give me a few good lines once in a while? Please? Or at least let me speak in my secret voice. Fat chance.

A lighted bare bulb, a ramshackle of peeling wallpaper, filthy dishes piled by the rusted pump, an empty whiskey bottle toppled on the table, and beside it a picture of Mrs. Burroughs. Oh God no, Diane sighs and shakes her head. Hank's on his annual bender-wake.

Once a year Hank goes over to the Archer's with a bottle, gets pissed to the gills and bemoans the loss of the greatest woman who ever lived, Mrs. Burroughs. And it's that time again, only it looks as if her father brought the bottle to Hank this year. Diane knows that the sickest sight in the world is Hank drunk, uncontrollably drunk, crying like a big helpless baby in his drink, then passed out and slumped over the table. If there *is* a sicker sight, it's when he slinks back the next day, tail between his legs, worrying his engineer's cap in both hands, apologizing until he's tongue-tied, his shame at the "little one's having seen Hank behave so." The third person doesn't help.

And there's his old smelly shirt on the mounted antlers, which she's sure are fake, either that or bought somewhere. If he's out trying to milk in that condition, she'd better help. Diane knows that what Hank needs is for someone, a strong woman, to take control of his life.

She goes out the door singing the theme song from an old TV show: "Wonder woman, wonder woman . . ."

II

Excepting his annual binges over at our place, the only time I can remember Hank losing control was on the hunting trip. (I'll just look around the back of the barn first.) Mom was dead set against me going hunting, but I cried and kept whimpering that Dad had promised I could go when I turned ten. So Mom finally gave in. I seldom cry but I know when it'll work.

Mom and Mrs. Burroughs packed this gigantic picnic basket and me and Hank and Dad set out before sunrise. We walked into the woods until the dew was burned off the grass. That's the woods that began where they're building the Bluewater Mall. We didn't see anything but a few squirrels and muskrats. I was getting impatient for something big to shoot at because they'd promised me that I could have the first shot. I thought they meant it too, though I worried about the way they kept winking at each other when I reminded them. We stopped to eat in a roomy clearing just when the pale day-moon was fading out directly overhead.

I was laying everything out perfectly when a fawn stuck its head out from behind some evergreen bushes not fifty feet away. I tried to grab Hank's rifle but he put it behind his back. I started screaming that they had promised me the first shot, but Hank kept fending me off with his big hands. He and Dad roared laughter. When I looked back to where the fawn had stood, I caught the hindquarters of a doe galloping into the bush. I just stood there trying my hardest not to cry, my throat all lumpy, hating Dad and Hank, but most of all Hank.

They ribbed me all through the meal but I didn't say a word. I couldn't speak or eat. My throat felt as dry and narrow as a piece of straw. After everything was packed into the basket, Hank pulled a bottle of whiskey from his big coat pocket. He sliced the seal with his gross thumbnail and held the bottle towards me: "Here, sweetheart, Hank will let you take the first shot . . . like a man!" And with that he and Dad started laughing uncontrollably again.

I didn't cry, though it drove me crazy having the wool pulled over my eyes like that. I sat on the ground at a good distance from them and closed my eyes. My head vibrated. When I opened my eyes I realized for the first time that I possessed the secret power of the go-away game. They didn't die, though. They got stinking drunk and lost their minds. Dad bragged that he was going to buy the McKenzie place. Hank bragged that he'd soon be needing the land where the new school now sits, what with the family he was planning.

At about three in the afternoon, the bottle empty, they lay flat on their backs and fell asleep, or passed out. I felt so cheated that I got up and decided to go home. When I turned to leave I spotted antlers at the same spot in the brush. Not a fawn or doe this time, a full-grown buck. He stood like an idiot just watching us, as if waiting for an invitation to join us. It's quite possible he was attracted by Dad's and Hank's snoring. I willed him to stay and he bowed to chomp some leaves. But I knew even then that that wasn't the way the game worked and that I'd better hurry.

Moving as quickly and as quietly as I could, I returned to where they were sleeping and ever so gently slipped Hank's rifle from under his leg. I sighted the buck's head along the barrel and started walking towards him, the gun against my shoulder, my finger on the trigger, repeating to myself, squeeze it don't jerk it, squeeze it don't jerk it. When the buck's mouth froze in mid-munch I squeezed the trigger. I dropped the rifle and went reeling backwards and fell on top of Dad, who was already jumping to his feet and shouting, "What the hell!" Hank was halfway to the buck, which was down on its buckled forelegs, head propped by its antlers, snout nuzzling the earth. It keeled over before Hank reached it and started making this crying sound like a baby.

Dad kept shouting like a raving lunatic, "It was loaded? It was loaded?"

But I felt great as Dad and I ran across to Hank and the buck, like I was floating. Just the slightest crooking of my finger could do *that*. I could see Dad and Hank—the big men—dying of embarrassment when I told everyone that I'd done the hunting while they were helplessly drunk.

Hank was on his knees, delicately turning the filthy snout in his hands to examine the wound in the buck's neck. Blood oozed onto the ground then spouted like a fountain when the wound was freed. What a shot! Shaking his head and breathing like someone about to have a conniption fit, Hank slid one of his big hands under the buck's head and stroked its neck. Its hind legs quivered like a dead frog's when you shock them.

Hank went back and got his rifle, returned and shot the buck in the head, right between its open vibrating eyes. Dad staggered off and threw up behind a tree. When Hank turned to me I was crying uncontrollably. He began crying silently too—for the stupid deer, I think. That was when I fell in love with Hank. I think I was crying because I realized that I'd just fallen in love. I had promised myself that I didn't want anything to do with goofy boys, or love. Too unpredictable. And there I was at ten years old, madly in love with an older, *married* man, and a man who cried like a woman at that! And there were Mrs. Burroughs and the unborn baby—the first victims of the go-away game.

Now *that's* funny. Where could he be? The lights aren't on in the barn, but he's got to be in there. He'd never leave the barn door open. And listen to all that barking. Hank's black mongrels going crazy about something. Ah the smell! Breathe deeply, Di dear. The milking stool toppled beneath Selly, her udder full and looking sore, poor thing. What are those mutts going nuts about at the loft ladder? . . . Good God! I know! He's drunk and sleeping it off in the loft. And the dogs are trying to tell him they're starved, or something.

"Hank?" This is going to be good. "Hennn-reee!" What lungs! What a voice! I wouldn't be at all surprised to find Dad up there with him, both of them pissed to the gills. But no, Dad would never have let Hank try to milk in that condition. So, Hank must have gone it alone this year. Another tradition shot to hell. Oh well, who gives a *fuck* any more? "Hennn-reee! Where are the eggs, dear?"

III

Blood. I never knew there would be so much blood. Butch Shehan left that part out. I knew it was supposed to hurt at first. But I never knew how much, or that it would feel so good after a while. I know I shouldn't have done it. No, I don't know that. I couldn't have stopped myself anyway. It was like I was drunk when I raised my head above the floor of the loft and saw him lying there stark naked, his thing cradled in his big hand. Everything changed. Just like that. I lost control. Yes, that's it. Like I was drunk and out of control.

I should have backed down the ladder and gone straight home. But when he opened his bloodshot eyes and said, "Alice, dear, dear Alice," I went to him, the poor dear, he looked so helpless. And when he reached up under my dress and touched me and said, "Are you coming to bed, dear Alice?" I dropped down beside him and laid my head on his chest. I heard his heart like thunder from a bad storm a few miles passed. His hands were so soft on my hair and neck, so gentle up and down my back. I just went crazy with love. I couldn't control it and I didn't want to.

I took off my clothes and just lay there beside him. I think I cried just a little. I was so gone I hardly knew *what* I was doing. It felt like there was a big white feather inside me running from my throat to my crotch, felt like it was twirling still like the Milky Way. I knew then that I was going to do it to him. I didn't care who he thought I was. I wasn't me anyway.

His hands were rubbing me all over, so my hands started doing the same to him. He said, "And when he grows . . . we'll make this place go . . . or a girl, a help to you . . ."

I was up in the beams looking down, saw my body lie on top of him for a moment, then roll off and lie by his side. That was a little scary, but I liked it too.

Then I couldn't see myself because he rested on all fours above me and with his eyes shut tightly asked, "It's safe? . . . Not too far along?" He was trying to put it in but kept missing.

I came down and let my hands reach and take hold of it. It felt three times bigger than it looked in the sex-ed diagrams, at least three times. It went in a little ways and I choked a scream. I wanted to stop right then because it hurt so much. But once it was in he started moving it back and forth and back and forth, mindlessly, like a sluggish machine. It began to hurt less. It began to feel good. Then so good that I was angry when he stopped. He rolled off and lay flat on his back, his eyes still closed. I knew he hadn't finished and I wanted it to last just a little longer. So I shook his shoulder.

He sputtered then whined, "Dear Alice, dear, dear . . . when are you coming . . ." His eyelashes batted like the teeth of an old-style mower: "Archer girl? . . . such a help to you since Hank . . ."

Not the third person, I gritted my teeth. I got madder and began shouting that Alice wanted it to last longer. Forget the fucking Archer girl! Just a little longer, please, before it's all over.

But I was too late. He started snoring like a power saw. I'm always too late for everything. I got up and started dressing, afraid that I'd now be too late for the Ball.

That's when I noticed the blood smeared down my thighs like the red oil Dad used to use to rustproof. I got scared. I hurried down the ladder, left the barn and ran to the dead centre of the new crossroads, the stink of Hanks' shitpiles and piss swamps caught in my nostrils. I stood there in a panic, staring at the rising harvest moon and trying to get control of myself. I willed myself to see the moon the way it looks at the beginning of those stupid werewolf movies, emerging from behind wispy clouds, a pure white ball dripping blood. I concentrated hard on the go-away game, but the full moon just hung there like a big mindless smile button. It seemed so near that I could reach out and scratch it. But I couldn't. I couldn't do anything any more. I could hardly breathe.

I started walking to my house. The nearer I got the more I hurried, until I was running. It wasn't until I stood outside our screen door that I realized I'd forgotten my fucking green leotards. Good riddance, I grinned, then started screaming. I kept screaming that Hank had raped me. I completely lost control and passed out.

I'm in perfect control now, though. Am I ever! Don't worry about me, kiddo. (Wait, that's not the way I talk.) The go-away game is again working like a charm. And I'm now the most popular girl at school . . . though I'm not back at school yet. Still, just about all the old crowd have been up to visit me, *dahling*. (Is that it? Fuck no.) Yesterday, a small intimate party organized by Pat Fletcher right here in my private room, a sort of send-off affair, *très chic*, as Miss Piggy would say. (*Now* we're rolling! I'm so excited, and I just can't hide it; I'm about to . . .) Pat looked meanly at Mike O'Reilly when he asked me how's life on the funny farm. The reference to Hank-the-hick-Burroughs' place almost ruined my get-well bash. That O'Reilly—*très gauche!* I patiently explained that I stopped the bleeding myself by ignoring the doctors and obeying the messages. O'Reilly pursed his lips at Debbie Summers, twirled a finger at his temple and called her cuck-oo. (*What!*) Pat took him out into the hall and told him to leave because it was my party and he shouldn't be flirting with that slutting cunt.

I also told Dr. Clayton that I'd stopped the bleeding, and he promised that if I'm good at the new hospital in St. Thomas I'd be out in no time! How he found out that it was me who caused that groping pisspot washer to slip . . . Well, it's beyond me. Or that it was *my* power that made the newspaper fall out of Dad's back pocket so I could read what they did to that pervert, Hank-the-hick-Burroughs . . . beats me. And *my* go-away game that caused the pervert to kill himself in the new funny farm they carted him off to . . . Proof of my power? Well, consider this: I had the crazy shit-farmer hang himself with his own filthy clothing, the very same clothes he was wearing . . . Ah, but the newspaper gave me no credit. (It's slipping away, I'm losing it.) It talked about me without even mentioning my name, as though I were a child who needed protecting. (Going . . .) I hope at least that the people who move into the new houses Clefton will build on the pervert's old stinking farm give me some credit. (going . . .) Or at least think of me once in a while, when they water *the* maple, say. (gone.)

But it's such a lonely responsibility, my power, such a burden. I can't risk sleeping at night, can't allow myself the luxury of the small white pills those nosey nurses force on me. Such a responsibility. I just lie here staring at the moon, straining to catch its waning messages, knowing that if I close my eyes for even a split second it will come crashing its high whiteness all over the world, on all that was mine, all that I love.

The Lumbs

I have been tangling with a directive which, when signed, will cause a collection of Orientals to be evicted from their seedy riverfront apartment. But Front Street must come down. The Petrosar Building will go up, with or without my approval as Chairman of Sarnia's Regional Planning Committee. So I sign "Thomas," then brood further. Should I include my middle initial, the sibilant S? Or should I sign my whole middle name? I smirk. And for no good reason the impersonal betrayal reminds me of the Lumbs.

"Now, Roderick Felix," hollered Daisy Lumb, "you too Mathew Norman and Frederick Thomas—and you cross your eyes again Eustace Earle and I'll gouge 'em out, I will—Leapin' Larry Shane's gonna win and that's that, and I'll bet Eustace Earle six pieces of honey-and-peanut-buttered toast . . ."

The Sheik had slipped something from the waistband of his black tights and was rubbing it into Leaping Larry's eyes. Leaping Larry dug both balled fists into his own eyes and stomped across the apron like a toddler, with those staggering spread-kneed crashing steps of the sumo wrestler. When he removed his fists to howl at the camera, the blood gushed from his eyes. The Sheik jumped him from behind and applied his signature Sleeper Hold. Leaping Larry lost consciousness, and the World Heavyweight Championship. The live audience went wild, the Lumbs went wilder.

Daddy Lumb pinched his personal TV guide from his face: "Leapin' Larry Shane lose?" He rolled up the TV guide, leaned forward and smacked the back of Eustace Earle's head, then fell back and knocked his own head on the couch's thin stiff arm. "Unacknowledged shiteing parts!" he shouted. Eustace Earle pointed at his Dad and laughed ecstatically.

I sat rigidly at the end of the couch, fighting the stink from Daddy Lumb's red thermal socks. My mother had some scheme in the works, and I feared I would no longer be sharing the Lumb obsession with wrestling. It was an unbearable situation: I wanted to explain my innocence, and to say good-bye. But I left the Lumbs as usual: stuffed with take-out food, laughed at for washing my hands, for brushing my teeth with my finger, and for asking permission to return for the next show.

The Lumb affair began when they were moved from Chatham to Sarnia. They were beneficiaries of our parish, which couldn't resist the pathetic feature in the *Sarnia Spectator:* "Family Of Eight Homeless, Arson Suspected." My mother made me accompany her to the church the Sunday afternoon the Lumbs arrived. Mom had to go, being the elected Chairman of the St. Stephen's Relief Committee, an *ad hoc* organization.

The welcoming delegation waited in the driveway between church and rectory: Father Jameson, Mrs. MacNeal (secretary), without her son and my classmate Danny, the O'Tooles and their seven busy kids, a few white-gloved women, and my prim mother, who continually pinched me closer.

"It's gotta be them this time!" Pat O'Toole screamed from the sidewalk. "It's the van Dad sold us!"

The baby-blue van careened into the driveway and, without reducing speed, barreled straight for the delegation. At the first shiver in Father Jameson's new black cassock, the entire group scattered like pigeons flung a handful of gravel. But the van came to a smooth stop about three feet from where Jameson had stood. We had all forgotten Daddy Lumb's blasphemous claim to be, as the *Spectator* reported, "the best goddamned trucker north of the forty-ninth."

I managed to slip my mother's hold as the committee sheepishly regrouped. I peeked from behind the O'Tooles to get a good look at this charity case. After all, the Lumbs were going to be *our* new neighbours.

Daisy Lumb was the first to alight. With hand outstretched and tilted downward like some kind of blade, she rolled dwarfishly towards the delegation, pillowy hips sliding up her sides with each step. She looked to be about two hundred pounds of tubular flesh stacked five feet high: in nylons turned down and knotted above the knees, in faded white print dress with strained side seams, in black pillbox hat that squatted squarely on her tiny knob of a head. Speck-framed glasses like a fancy masquerade mask rested atop puffed cheeks and magnified magnificently startled eyes.

Daddy Lumb sort of trailed then hid behind her. But *he* was tall and muscular, wearing a rumpled grey suit and a Detroit Tigers baseball cap. Daddy Lumb's mature matinee-idol looks, coupled with Daisy's dumpiness, were to become a source of mystery and jealous humour to Mom and Mrs. MacNeal. "That hunk with that lump," Mom said to Mrs. MacNeal on the phone that very afternoon. She turned redder when she spotted me by the door. But I was surprised only by the thought of Mom finding another woman's husband attractive.

In the church driveway, my mother began her welcoming speech: "On behalf of the St. Stephen's Relief Committee, I, Margaret Fleming, Chairman, would like to welcome you to Sarnia and our humble . . ."

Daisy went straight for the priest, took his hand and commenced pumping: "Father Fleming, you don't know what all you've done for us Lumbs. As I was sayin' to Wilma Eunice on the way down, 'That priest ee-is God's own shepherd.' That's what I said, didn't I? . . . Wilma Eunice?"

"She dee-id, Father Fleming," a girl's voice called from the van. "And then *I* said—" There was a thump from inside the van, which rocked as a cane snapped against the windshield.

A touch discomposed, my mother began her first of many vain attempts to correct Daisy Lumb: "Pardon me, Mrs. Lumb— *it is Mrs. Daisy Lumb?*—but *I* am Margaret Fleming. This is our parish priest, Father . . ."

Smiling distractedly at Mom as though humouring an insistent child, Daisy turned and hollered at the van, "Lumbs!"

Daddy Lumb stepped forward and grasped Mom's hovering hand: "That was a *fine* speech, Mrs. Margaret." He stepped back behind his wife as the Lumb children literally came tumbling out of the van in a tangle of wrestling holds. Mom spotted me with her Svengali eyes and made the wormy little vein dance behind the skin of her forehead.

Roderick Felix was the first to disengage and step forward, though not before turning and kicking Eustace Earle in the ribs. "Cobo Hall!" he roared. "The cage!" He wore a filthy cast on his right forearm and walked with his head tilted slightly backwards and his chin thrust upward, because his back was slightly bowed. Although my age, he was a good head taller and a good fifty pounds heavier. Wilma Eunice was next, with a cane, her left leg thinner and paler than the right; then Matthew Norman, the picture of snobbish constraint in his dirty-white orthopedic collar; Frederick Thomas—a foot cast; Eustace Earle, apparently healthy; and last and least, little Luellen Barbara, a tissue of scabs and bruises. Arms stiff at their sides, exaggerating the lift of their knees, the Lumbs marched to form a line of descent from their father's side.

Mom again attempted her welcome: "We hope you, uh, Lumbs can find room in the goodness of your hearts to accept this, *our* offer to lighten your burden in these, your days of darkness. Fire, as Father Jameson can tell you, is a symbol of purgation and conversion. I—"

"Eus-tace Earle," Daisy barked, "front and centre." And there was as much authority in the way she cracked the order as in my mother's dancing worm.

Eustace Earle slid a half-step and had to be prodded forward by Wilma Eunice's cane. "W-W-W—"

Daisy reached back and cuffed him. "Lumbs, how many times am I a-going to tell you: there ain't nothin' funny about a stammer. Now continue Eustace Earle."

"We are g-g-grateful to F-Father J-J-J-Jameson an-an-an' all—"

"That'll be all, Eustace Earle," commanded Daisy. "Thank *you* on behalf of the Lumbs gathered here today for that fine fee-itting oration. Again, on behalf of the Lumbs," and she sang, "I tha-an-kyou." She shoved Eustace Earle back on top of little Luellen Barbara.

"Shiteing parts!" Luellen Barbara screamed. She hopped about on one foot and wailed: "It's fractured! Ten-to-one it's broken! I'll bet I need a cast!"

Daisy pinched little Luellen Barbara on the upper arm, glared at Wilma Eunice and threatened a general backhand. Daddy Lumb cowered. Wilma Eunice snatched Luellen Barbara by the nape of the neck and hobbled to the van.

Daisy mugged apologetically at the priest, cupped, lifted and shifted her massive breasts. She spoke to Mom for the first time: "We likes, you see, to make Eustace Earle do the talkin' for the Lumbs because he stee-ill needs work on his impediment. As a mother I'm sure you understand."

"Why, he did just splendidly for a—"

"You promised you wouldn't here!" Eustace Earle ran to the van.

"Eustace Earle, you get your Lumb ass out here this instant!" Daisy slapped her plump cheek and rolled her great eyes: "Eu-stace Earle Lumb, wee-ill you please get your Lumb bum out here."

Roderick Felix was dispatched to fetch Eustace Earle. Mat-thew Norman was ordered to go and see what was taking "them

Lumbs" so long. He stiffened to attention, clicked his heels, and held a German salute as he goose-stepped to the van. Daisy shrieked laughter and momentarily collapsed against Daddy Lumb, until he staggered. Then Daisy, Father Jameson and Mom stood smiling and agreeing with one another: It was indeed a long drive from Chatham, a humid day (Daisy said, "A real scorcher for the vaginal rash on little Luellen Barbara's private parts"), and, yes, it would be a relief to get settled in.

"Of course," mused Daisy, "Little Luellen Barbara was already watching the TV when she was but eight weeks old. She got the brains in the Lumb Family."

"This lady," said Mom, grown confident again, "is Mrs. Verna MacNeal, vice-president. And this is Mrs. Teresa O'Toole, treasurer, *our* treasure, as we like—"

"We dropped the O from our name generations back," said Daisy as she turned away. I saw her wink at Daddy Lumb. "Frederick Thomas, you and Daddy Lumb go and see what ee-is taking that crowd of Lumbs."

"Well then," sighed Daisy after a short pause, "I suppose we should all get a move on . . . and so . . ."

And so Daisy swaggered back to the van.

Father Jameson begged off with the lame excuse of having to deliver communion to shut-ins. Mrs. MacNeal's convenient memory conjured up a hospital visit to an ailing nun. The O'Toole kids simply broke rank and ran screaming. "They're Irish?" Mrs. O'Toole said to her husband as they walked away. The other ladies, looking encumbered suddenly by their shiny plastic purses, dispersed without excuses, the purses snapping smartly as the good white gloves were stowed for a more rewarding outing.

In the Lumbs' driveway, Mom stared straight through the windshield. The worm was embossed on her forehead as she calmly said that I could run along now. "No call for both of us to witness *this*." But there was no way I was going anywhere.

The Lumbs trooped forth: Daddy Lumb with a picnic cooler, Roderick Felix with a card table, Wilma Eunice with a fiery red pot big enough to boil a missionary in, the younger brothers with folding chairs, and little Luellen Barbara with three TV guides hugged to her chest. They lined up as my mother struggled with the new brass lock on the side door.

"Let me have a go, Mom, it opened easy last night."

She turned and kicked me on the shin. We stared at each other in disbelief.

"A match!" shouted little Luellen Barbara.

"A match?" said Eustace Earle, and he tossed a book of matches on the ground between Mom and me.

A few of the Lumbs snickered, but Daddy Lumb pinched Eustace Earle aside and gave him a whispered dressing down.

Daisy oohed and ahed over the house. "Isn't it a sight, Lumbs? Youse are all, Mrs. Margaret, all of youse, God's own instruments of salvation to provide this mercy for these weary Lumb eyes. If you so much as provide yeast for the best of my children, as the book says. Isn't that right, Eustace Earle?"

Daisy threw a tricky eye sideways. The older Lumbs again snickered.

"I-I-I-I—" Eustace Earle stuttered like a sailor until he was kicked on the ankle by his mother.

Instead of the orderly tour my mother had planned, the Lumbs scurried to reconnoitre in what was more an invasion and occupation. The nutritionally stocked fridge was ignored for the big red pot to boil their own wieners. The dining-room set ("Rather used, but serviceable," as Mom had described it to Mrs. MacNeal) received further neglect in favour of the card table. Roderick Felix barrelled for the TV. He tore the kids' TV guide from a screaming and scrappy little Luellen Barbara, who spat on my mother's hand when she bent and said, "There-there, ch—"

Roderick Felix bellowed, "Holy shiteing parts, Lumbs! There's wrestling on *three* different channels here!"

The clattering kitchen silenced. Then a louder racket from all rooms as the Lumbs scrambled into the living room and fought for position in front of the TV.

Mom climbed halfway up the stairs to the second floor, tore down the "Welcome Lovely Lumbs" banner, and crumpled it. She poked her gritty smile into the living room: "Well, then, I will send Tommy over this evening to see how your are getting acquainted with your new . . . setting."

Daisy, engrossed by the wrestling show, lifted an arresting pudgy hand: "Tom-mee . . . Thomas?" She wasn't satisfied until the Sheik pinned Gorgeous George's shoulders for the three-count. She leaned forward on the ottoman, turned down the volume, and heaved to her feet. "I'll bet you that A-rab's a comer! Leaping Larry Shane had best practice his mares." With upturned hands she gestured like a priest for the Lumbs to rise.

They lined up from Daddy Lumb to little Luellen Barbara and, conducted by Daisy, sang: "We thank you, we thank you, we tha-an-kyou." Daisy nodded dismissively in my mother's direction, cranked up the volume, and knocked Eustace Earle a clout that toppled him from her seat. Daddy Lumb threw an expert scissors around Eustace Earle's neck, pinned him and groaned, "Someone count!" Daisy hit the floor on her knees, and propped on one elbow, with her cheek to the floor so she could see if Eustace Earle's shoulders cleared it, smacked a "One, two, three, out!"

Mom was rattled. She had to pinch me from the living-room archway and poke me out the front door. These Lumbs were something else entirely, no doubt about that.

That evening I watched Leaping Larry Shane come back from apparent unconsciousness and, with a barrage of Flying Mares that would have taken the head of a lesser champ, dethrone Bo-Bo Brazil. Lord Athel Layton, the host of Big Time Wrestling and former British heavyweight champion of the world, presented Leaping Larry with Bo-Bo's gilded world championship belt.

Cause for celebration. Daddy Lumb was dispatched to Kentucky Fried Chicken. The blue and green tractor of his eighteen-wheeler came roaring back in no time, black exhaust streaming into the evening from dual perpendicular side exhausts like silver wings. He drove over the curb and parked right on the front lawn, the same lawn that Mom had made me trim the day before, though I had trimmed it only three days before that. I didn't know how he'd materialized the head of a truck, but it wouldn't wash on

Cameron Street. Ours was a quiet street, a shadowy street, a street so narrow that the road sloped sharply to the curbs, the maples meshing so thickly above that I could walk down the crest of the road during a light rain and not get wet.

Daisy didn't bother asking if I cared to join them, she just served me. "I'll bet you he ee-is the greatest, that Leapin' Larry Shane," she managed, a slice of Grecian bread almost all in her mouth. "But that new Sheik fella? . . ."

We ate in front of the TV, with the empty chicken bucket on top of the set. According to the conditions of our bet, the one who missed the bucket most often was obliged to clean up the mess of bones and make instant coffee and brown-sugared toast for everyone. The Lumbs were fanatical betters. Just about every statement was prefaced by, "I'll bet you."

"I'll bet you I've been wearing my underwear longer than you," Matthew Norman once baited Eustace Earle.

"I-I-I'll b-b-b—"

"I'll bet you Matthew Norman's wearing *long* johns!" Roderick Felix said loudly. I don't think that Roderick Felix would normally have come to Eustace Earle's rescue. From the way he had eyed me sideways as he made his unLumb-like joke, I suspected that my presence was interfering with their sport.

The Lumbs roared their laughter, all faces turned to me, mouths wide open and displaying chewed toast. Eustace Earle dumped the card table, grabbed Matthew Norman's last piece of toast and ran. Little Luellen Barbara set up a scream because her sugar-coated, coffee-soaked cereal had been spilled down her front as she was tilting the bowl to her face. Daddy Lumb fell of his chair from laughing so hard. I stood in a corner by the adults' table, waiting for Roderick Felix to finish, wishing that I was allowed to drink coffee. Roderick Felix and Wilma Eunice didn't look stunted in their growth to me.

But that first night that we ate the sweet chicken, Daisy said, "Five-to-one for chocolate hale on saltines that Killer Ricki Cortez takes down Man Mountain before the two-minute mark of the second. Any takers? . . . *Babies.*"

Eustace Earle sneaked a hand towards his mother's TV guide; without taking her eyes off the TV, she sent him sprawling with a knee to the chin.

It wasn't until the macaroni salad went round that they acknowledged my first tentative bet of plain toast. I cheered Dick the Bruiser to victory, then graciously accepted my winnings from Wilma Eunice, my temporary and magnanimous servant. She had thoughtfully covered my toast with sliced peaches and cinnamon sugar. Daisy crowned me with the chicken bucket and paraded me about the living room to a Lumb humming of "Pomp and Circumstance." Wilma Eunice curtsied.

A few times I attempted vainly to point out to the Lumbs the contradictory fact that each of the three stations they now received had its own world champions, single, tag-team, and midget, both sexes. But they all insisted (all but Eustace Earle) that Leaping Larry Shane was the only true world champion. The midgets weren't for real, of course. It was a matter of common Lumb knowledge that the midget bouts were fixed so that the shorter or, in the event of even height, more disproportioned contender won, the truer dwarf. Like the Relief Committee emissaries who occasionally dropped by, the midgets were viewed as a kind of comic relief from the real sport, warranting only howls of derision when they left the scene.

"I'll bet everyone knows that Mike the Mighty Mite's always gonna win," said Matthew Norman, "'cause he's got a polio arm, too."

"I-I-I'll b-b-b-b—" But I never learned whether Eustace Earle shared his family's scepticism with respect to the midget bouts, because he was cut short by his father's heel on the back of his neck.

The day after their arrival, I waited for Roderick Felix three blocks from school. I asked him how he could believe that it *all* wasn't fixed when there could be any number of champions. It stood only to reason.

"Don't be so stupid," he spat, picking at the permanent scabs on the bridge of his nose. He thrust his chin: "Ain't there a bunch of champions in every division of boxing? Ain't there a world champion of baseball in Japan as well as the Tigers?" ("Taggers," he pronounced it. The way they talked, with their "stee-ills" and "wee-ills," the Lumbs sounded like a Canadian version of hillbillies.) "Ain't there a Grey Cup and an NFL champion? Everybody does it. There's a million different lists of the number one record. That stuff don't mean unwiped shiteing parts. . . . God, and you're *supposed* to be the smartest kid in our class." (Roderick Felix could surprise and humiliate me like that.) "And how come you stood on that MacNeal weakling's side and cheered for him when he said I stunk?"

Mom had insisted that I walk with Roderick Felix the first few days, never mind that she'd refused to offer Daisy a second cup of coffee her first morning in Sarnia. Mom had mused aloud the night of the Lumbs' arrival that *we* must treat them like Christians, though she no longer suggested that Roderick Felix and I might become best friends, seeing as how we were the same age, as she'd seen previous to the Lumbs' arrival.

Returning from my first evening with the Lumbs, I was startled by my mother sitting alone on our screened-in back porch. I could hear my father's Glenn Miller music. That meant he was tuning her out.

"Well?" she asked, lighting a cigarette off the butt of the previous one. My mother drank and smoked only when under stress, as when she'd been forced to let Mrs. MacNeal have a go at the failing bingo confectionery, or when Dad had made her let me go camping with the O'Tooles.

"They're okay, I guess. They just pigged-out on Kentucky Fried Chicken, though."

"I hope, for your sake, young man, that you did not eat any of that . . . that *trash*. And what *were* you doing over there for so long?"

"I was helping them, like you told me to."

"And all that perfectly good meat in their fridge freezer. . . . Well, your supper is in the oven, Tommy."

"I'm not hungry."

"Did you—"

"Naw, I'm just not—"

"*Naw?*"

"No, Mom."

"Did you . . . did you show them where Verna MacNeal put the clothes?"

"Yeah, and some of them smell pretty funny."

"What *precisely* do you mean, Tommy, by *funny?*"

"I dunno, kinda damp and smelly like the inside of a skate."

"Tommy, I want you to promise me something, and it will be just for a short duration—God willing—though you would think people could show a little more Christian tolerance. . . ."

Three weeks later, I was lying on my back and slapping the Lumbs' living-room floor, struggling to escape Wilma Eunice's Tasmanian Toe-hold. I had to admit she was right, to all the assembled and cheering Lumbs: it was true, even a girl could do it, it was real, I was twice wrong, and yes, the more I struggled the more entrapped I became. Oh yes, yes, yes! (What I never revealed was how strangely handled I felt wrestling with the sweating Wilma Eunice, and how little I fought to free myself from the recovered thigh that pinned my heaving chest.) There was a knock at the front door, followed by the entrance of Uncle Bernard Winston and his daughter, Jacqueline Elizabeth. Lumbs, the two of them, judging by their white-skinned plumpness. All Lumbs had skin as pale as peeled potato, unwashed.

"She's left me again," Uncle Bernard Winston beamingly sighed. He held his suitcase like a football and danced through the sprawled Lumbs, who ignored him. I, on the other hand, made to tackle him and landed atop Wilma Eunice, who bounced me like a midget.

"Dibs on Killer Kawolski!" shouted Jacqueline Elizabeth as she slid to a place in front of the TV.

The uncle sat on the arm of the couch, accepted the hand Daisy placed on his knee, and merely nodded when she said gloomily, "Leaping Larry Shane had best stay out of the cage. I'll bet he's gonna lose his belt to The Pummeling Pollack."

But he didn't, costing me fifteen minutes in the Lumbs' kitchen to prepare a heaping plate of grilled cheese sandwiches sprinkled with chocolate hale and powdered with icing sugar. I had been set up by Daisy. As Wilma Eunice patiently pointed out, how could I have expected Kawolski to emerge victorious? *His* most recent cage match with Bo-Bo Brazil had cost him even more dearly than had Leaping Larry's cage match win over Fritz Von Hilter (who was the Sheik's tag-team partner). Kawolski wore an orthopedic collar, a cast on his wrist, and a knee brace. Wilma Eunice gently applied pressure to my hand resting contentedly in her Knuckle Crusher. "You'll learn," she whispered and smiled a smile that curled my toes. "Ouch," I whispered.

"You don't wanna bet with *these* Lumbs when it comes to wrestling," Uncle Bernard Winston winked. "They'll skin ya alive."

Roderick Felix joined the flailing: "And I'll bet you, Uncle Bernard Winston, that Thomas . . . What's your middle name, Thomas?"

"Uh, Stearns. I'm named after my mother's favourite—"

"And I'll bet you by best friend, Thomas Stearns, is *supposed* to be the smartest in our class." Roderick Felix beamed at Uncle Bernard Winston.

The uncle pursed his lips in an air whistle. Wilma Eunice tore her grilled cheese and gave the bigger half to me. It hurt to swallow.

Others Lumbs arrived over the following week: Uncle Bernard Winston's two older children, Angelica Fidelity Grace and Charles Andrew John-John; Daddy Lumb's cousin on his father's side, Archibald Reginald Alexander (so that there were now two trailorless tractors parked on the front lawn, which had grown around the tractors like open savannah); and Aunt Trix, Uncle Bernard Winston's briefly estranged wife (Trix, I suppose, because she, like the truncated Daisy, was not a blood Lumb). And more. By the end of the month, there were twenty people living in the little white house next door, sleeping in the kitchen, in the bathtub, in a tent on the front lawn. And the rent was due from the Relief Committee.

"You are spending too much time over there, Tommy," my mother said as she hurried out of the kitchen with a plate of tooth-picked cheese and pickled onions.

"Thomas," I called.

She returned and stood with her forefinger to her chin. "Now let me see: Father Jameson, the MacNeals, the O'Tooles, Alderman Sadhi and his companion. That should do it."

"Do what? An' whadyamean, too much time over there?"

"Don't *you* start speaking like *them*, young man. *You* have been brought up to speak the queen's English." She reached to the ashtray for a long-ashed cigarette, paused, and butted it out instead: "No matter, never mind. If all goes as planned tonight, they'll be somebody else's worry next month."

"Excuse me."

"Lookit me!" she shrieked and bolted, removing and cramming her apron into the silverware drawer of the buffet. She called from the stairs: "And you be home by ten tonight, Tommy."

"But tonight's the rematch between Leaping Larry Shane and the Sheik for the heavyweight championship of the whole world. And before that, Bo-Bo Brazil's taking on eight white midgets all at the same time!"

"Well, okay, but no later than ten. And get something out of the fridge for yourself." She was upstairs: "But don't you dare touch the mousse!"

Don't touch the Moose! I tried to imagine my mother roaring those words while stabbing a finger at Lord Athel Layton's chest. I couldn't.

"There's a restaurant," I hollered, twisting my neck as we drove past. I kneaded the nape.

"Did Wilma Eunice hurt your neck in the leg scissors, Thomas Stearns?" Roderick Felix asked. "We gotta lotta spare collars."

"Well, maybe I could try it just at your place."

Roderick Felix turned and thrust his chin at me: "I'll bet *you* don't even know *why* KFC's fries are better than any restaurant's?"

"Beats me." Such distinctions were still revelation to me. But why this sudden spoiling for a fight? Was it because at class Confessions that morning I'd ignored the vacant space of pew Roderick Felix had patted?

Roderick Felix turned to his father and they shouted at each other, "There's more of 'em!"

Roderick Felix turned and shouted at me, "And they're *not* all dry and floury!"

Fine by me! I felt on top of the world, my first time in the truck. And I'll bet you it was a special favour, as Daisy had told me when I chipped two dollars into the food kitty.

"The Mrs. says there's some sort of to-do at your place tonight," Daddy Lumb remarked offhandedly. "Father Jameson, the mayor, and all them from the church that helped us Lumbs see our way clear."

"Yeah."

"I'll bet you they're fixin' to give the Lumbs the ol' heave-ho now that Eustace Earle's home from the burn unit," he whispered.

"Na." But I felt them both glance sideways and had to turn to my window. "There's an A&W!"

Daddy Lumb ground the gears: "Unacknowledged shiteing parts! . . . Ah well, it's been done before, son."

I felt Roderick Felix staring at the back of my head. "Fries too small." I knew his head was level for once, his lips wet and pouting in that way he seldom betrayed. "I'll bet *you* they're gonna give us Lumbs something else," he shouted, spraying the back of my neck. I turned slightly to catch his faint reflection in my window. "Wilma Eunice says one of those great big aerials. Is she right, Thomas Stearns?" He was almost whimpering. "Is she, Thomas Stearns? Is she right?"

"You *bet* she is, Rod—friend," I whispered at my faint face.

I lost that bet. The next day the Lumbs were gone. Without a good-bye. "Neither a by-your-leave nor so much as a thank you kindly,

like thieves in the night," as my mother informed Mrs. MacNeal on
the phone that morning. "They must have smelled it coming. She
could have left that looker of a husband, though."

I listened to Mom's side of the conversation from the dining-
room table, my stomach fisting at the sight of the dry shredded
wheat she expected me to eat. "Ain't there even no raisins in this
place?" I shouted. She ignored me.

"He did! . . . He didn't?" She poked her smug and flushed
face round the corner: "Tommy, did that big Lumb galloot try to
choke Danny MacNeal?"

"I'll bet you it was a Half-Nelson."

"Pardon *me*, young man?"

"I'll bet you Daniel started it by saying that Roderick Felix
stunk all the time and was stupid and had no friends here."

"Tommy! How many times *must* you be told? This is *not* a
casino."

"Yes, he did, but Roderick Felix let Danny pin him for a
while, he was just playing. Have you ever seen the muscles on that
guy!" I don't know why—I didn't feel at all like crying—but my
breath came in catches.

"And you didn't help your best friend?" The worm stirred
behind the skin on her forehead. "Well, shame on you." She
stepped out of sight: "Good for your Danny, that'll show them
their place."

I played hooky that day, the first and only time I ever would.
I walked along the St. Clair River, from the Imperial Oil docks to
the Sarnia Marina. The broken cement blocks of former docks
were covered with green slime like filthy teeth chipped in some
prehistoric battle, rainbows of oil near shore gleamed like KFC
juice on a sun-struck chin, the unpainted backs of the Front Street
stores stared drably. I was angry that I had to be careful of my good
shoes and creased slacks . . . while something like a sick hunger
burned through me. I wanted to take my left forefinger and break
it sideways, or pull out a clump of hair and scalp, something! . . .
Lonely, though I'd never really considered Roderick Felix a friend.
I didn't know exactly what he'd been, but I couldn't imagine

introducing him to anyone in the real world as "My best friend, Roderick Felix Lumb." And Wilma Eunice. Two days before we had wrestled alone in the long grass of their backyard while the Lumbs pigged-out inside. I had let her take me in the Full Nelson and drive my face into the sweet grass, my nose drilling the dirt. Then to my surprise I had pinned her easily and not let her up till she agreed that men were stronger. We had lain on our backs and laughed fitfully, then comfortably, and loosely held hands. I made up my mind to kiss her next time.

As I walked upstream along the river, the sun flashed across the shabby Front Street stores and sparkled on the blue-green rainbows of oil. I started to sniffle. Embarrassed and unable to control myself, I ran. For no good reason, I thought it would be all right to cry if hidden behind the two massive piles of the Riverfront Gravel Yard, an area that was strictly off-limits to all the kids I knew. Years ago, a twelve-year-old boy had been smothered under a landslide of gravel. Or so we were told, though the boy's age had been increasing as we grew older.

I picked up a rusted piece of corrugated iron used for building cement forms. I sat on the bank and with my good shoes skimming the river drew an arrow-pierced heart in the dirt. Inside it I wrote "TSF & WEL," then ran the iron rod around the heart till the whole was a messy circle. I threw the rod as far out in the river as I could and stared after it, foolishly thinking that the strong current might carry it downstream. I cried convulsively, as I have since only at the death of someone I loved, my father, my mother.

I set pen to directive and for the first time in my life sign my full middle name. It is within neither my province nor my power to look after *every*— I'll contact the Salvation Army, they can do something for that Vietnamese family. . . . But I can hear Daisy: "Thomas Stearns, would you like a leg or a breast this round?" . . . Unacknowledged shiteing parts! I'll go down to the river myself.

Floating

I am wandering about my three-room apartment, drifting from window to window, ashtray to ashtray, listing a bit. When I'm hungover, as I certainly am this Sunday morning (make that midday), I move anxiously like this from room to room, looking for something, for nothing, chain-smoking and trying like hell to remember what I said or did the night before that's going to cost me what's left of my future. (I *what?* I suggested to Professor Singleton that the paper he'd just published in *Critical Quarterly* must have been what he'd really been working on when he prepared the paper he'd just given in the faculty lounge? And that's not all?... Many choice items of that calibre.) But on this day after, the synapses are flooded still with kind alcohol. Nowadays I don't begin to feel really bad till the evening. The delayed pain and these Alzheimers hangovers are recent developments. But *surely* twenty-five is too young to have passed the full stroke of a drinking career that was just beginning to feel its hops. I've just begun truly letting go, dancing with potted palms in the grad club, insulting in a slur that alone insults any listener, that sort of thing. Coming up for air at 10 p.m. and thinking, Hey, where are the guys my age? Where are my old drinking buddies? Teaching where? Gone where? Married to whom? Submerging. I must say it, I can no more not say it than I can stop drinking beer: I've gotta quit drinking.

As I pass through my bedroom doorway a memory bubble begins nudging up through the mire of my mind (about to pop with a spray of some further smelly indiscretion), but Wanda Stuart's thrilled squawk saves me from the dank memory:

"I float so easily it's unbelievable!"

Oh yes, Wanda, of course you do, of course it is. *Your* incredulous floating is a fucking bonafide miracle! I wade cautiously to the window, thankful for this hated diversion, and peep down. There she is, with her rear wedged into the little inner-tube from Ronald's Volkswagen Rabbit, her arms dangling in the water and her legs splayed, and her pregnant belly soaking in the rays. She looks like some sort of floating insect . . . an earwig! An earwig drowning in a toilet, on its back and trying vainly to crawl up an illusive shaft of urine. And there's the bubble breaking surface tension—*Pop:* I did that to an earwig last night. These ersatz revelations are never as shattering as I anxiously anticipate.

Ronald, Wanda's husband, is sitting in a deck chair and sipping ice-tea with the Sunday paper hiding his all-too-hideable face. "Honey," he calls, his British accent clipping the syllables like a queer and compulsive gardener, "I am not altogether convinced that you should be in the pool today. The PH reading was not at all encouraging this morning." Don't you just love new pool owners?

"Oh Ronnie," she drawls. "Jimminy Crickets, can't I do nothin'?" When Wanda is irritated in the least by Ronald, she affects a Southern nasal twang that makes the gang on Hee-Haw sound like the graduates of a school of elocution.

But no, Wanda, honey, now that you've asked the question, you can*not* do anything. Nothing but bitch and complain. And lately it takes little enough to get her screeching up into my bedroom, where I am forced to try to work since the university cut me adrift, gave my office—my slip, my anchorage—to an incoming graduate student, a female and a foreigner who must pay higher tuition. You get my drift. They are so tactful, those academics: "Dear Students: Due to recent economizing measures, we are unable to support Ph.D. candidates beyond their sixth year.

Please be advised that we can no longer provide you with office space and photocopying privileges." The note was handwritten by our Chairman, a man without a Ph.D.

How, I asked the Chairman, is one to be expected to complete within six years one's thesis on the child in post-WWII British fiction (tentatively entitled "Father Of The Man/Man Of The Father: The Child in Post-WWII British Fiction") when one has been refused a teaching assistantship and deprived of office space and photocopying privileges? But he doesn't listen. No-no. *That* would require concentration. *That* would require him to remain the full half-hour he spends in his office three times a week. Besides he hates me.

Once when a group of us were drinking in the grad club, I half-jokingly questioned his disinterest as an administrator by complaining about the number of foreigners recently come into *our* graduate program. You see, the Chairman has mixed blood— European, Asian—coursing through his vengeful veins (may he stroke), so he favours all manner of Slavs, Latins, and Orientals. I drunkenly slobbered that it appeared as though our department would become a veritable ark for various boat peoples. I suspect I may then have opened wide my mouth and laughed round the table like a jackass. Of course the Chairman laughed, he had to, the snivelling shitbag. But he's never forgotten (though I'd thought the whining old mongrel was also sheets enough to the wind to rig a tall ship) and has held it against me. People never forgive.

I should get my cassette recorder and tape this bickering between the Stuarts, just to show the old unforgiving bum-boy the conditions under which I now have to work. Or some night I should record one of the Bacchanalias hosted by my Italian land-lords downstairs. Now *there's* noise. I can't hear myself think. Even the earwigs start losing their grip and falling from snug curtain linings.

"I think," Wanda says (and note the pretense), "that the more you swim in it, the less dirt gets in! Because I noticed after your students swam, *that one time*, it was really really cleaned up!"

Quick, someone call Bertrand Russell, a new form of logic is a-whelping, really.

From my window I can see Ronald's face, which is hidden from the drifting Wanda, implode in a mandarin cringe of Lucky Jim dimensions. "Honey," he manages as if speaking past a lemon wedged into his nostrils, "can you *possibly* be forgetting your delicate condition? We can't have the whole world polluting our pool. And mind you don't exert yourself."

"Oh Ron," Wanda pouts, letting her head loll back. She knits her fingers on the mound of her stomach and sort of hugs it closer, that stomach with all the definition of a dominant sea lion, and with one of those repulsive protruding bellybuttons. "Will you leave me alone. First you didn't want the baby bacause we couldn't afford it, then you'd only have it if we moved to Calgary-Alberta, because people out there could afford your stupid music lessons, then I had to promise to go back to work. And now I can't do *anything!* For Jeezuz sake, will you stop bellyachin'. 'Sides, I'm not swimming, just floatin'."

"Enough, Blanche, enough. The neighbours." Ronald snaps his paper, drops it beside the chair, leans forward and begins pulling at his wispy goatee. "And do you think any of those factors have altered one wit. Do you see any new students beating down our door? Unlike yourself, the business is barely staying afloat." Ronald smiles at his witticism. And is encouraged: "Why, if it were not for these dago accordion afficionados I'd be squeezed—"

"Stop it!" Wanda shouts at the sky. "Just stop this right now! . . . Please?"

Wanda doesn't know that Ronald is now examining her. She drifts with her hands and feet trailing in the water, shouting her defiance at the perfectly blue sky. In the mirroring pool she resembles some placidly gliding bird. A gull? A stork? But her complacency is unfair to poor Ronald. I pity the guy.

Ronald works from about noon till nine, every day, six days a week. He's a music teacher—"Ronald Stuart's Academy of Music: Piano, Violin, Guitar, Accordion," his sign reads. But it may as well read paper-and-comb and accordion, for all the piano, guitar, and violin players he instructs. The neighbourhood is located in the east end of London (Ontario), one of the poorer sections of this wealthy waspish city. The neighbourhood is inhabited by well-entrenched immigrants, Italians mostly. The old Italian couple I live above (thank God for spatial imagery) has a daughter residing next door and a son living across the street. The children's houses are replicas of this one: all three are garishly painted post-war houses with new iron-railed cement porches and freshly cemented driveways. The daughter has four children, the son six. The rest of the neighbourhood is the same, small clans reproducing and spreading like the concentric waves of a disturbed pool, or like waspgobblers leapfrogging from a mutated gene pool. And the colours of the houses! Yellow, orange, pistachio, mauve—enough to give a Canadian vision trouble. Once a month all the neighbourhood families get together at one home and live it up, in a manner of speaking. At these collective monthlies there are usually four or five accordion players, all of them squeezing out the sort of music that convinces all but the tone-deaf (make that the deaf) that the waters of Venice cannot rise too quickly. Once in a while some wine-soaked Latin will spring clumsily from his chair and do something completely idiotic, like twirl one of the startled-to-heart-attack black-clad women, or dance alone in a pitiable immitation of Anthony Quinn's Zorba (which, I know, is pitiable enough). And here's the observation that really burns the old orbs: they *know* they're behaving like beaker-full-of-the-warm-South stereotypes! They know it! Yet they persist! . . . Still, they *are* Ronald's only source of income. He knew what he was doing when he moved into this neighbourhood a year ago. You would be squeezed indeed to find such a pool of potential accordion players in Calgary-Alberta, as Wanda would slur it.

But for all his fortuitous market acumen, at the beginning of this summer Ronald committed a damning sin of omission: he hired a professional contractor to put in his swimming pool. Ronald didn't take account of your average Italian's passion for pouring cement. Cement pouring is a religious ceremony with

Italians. You can see and hear it in the borderline religious joy they
display when building yet another front porch or pouring another
driveway—pleasures, please observe, that they reserve for Sun-
days. I don't know if it's the expense that keeps them away from
the professional rip-off artists, or if it's the clannish, communal
way they live in this neighbourhood, but a "cement-a-pour" is *not*
something you contract outside the community. Even I could have
told Ronald that. His ignorance of local custom was the kiss of
death for his Academy, and I won't be a bit surprised if he wakes
up one of these mornings to find a fish floating belly up in his pool.
Ah yes, many a future accordion lesson got the cement overcoat
treatment in the glances the neighbours threw Ronald's way that
day the big contractor's truck backed its alien snout down his
gravelled driveway. I remember looking out my front window
and seeing a circle of our male neighbours jabbering away across
the street, their shoulders pinched, tossing their heads in the
direction of Ronald's house and gesticulating with uplifted palms
in affronted disbelief. The only "word" I could make out was
"Omina," that all-purpose Anglo-Italian verb: "Omina do this. . .
Omina tell him a ting." But I didn't need to hear, I knew what they
were deciding: Omina take my Salvadore out of his musical
academy ana send him to the music students at the big school. The
"big school" is the University of Western Ontario, which phrase
they give something of the exotically sexual. I like that, the
immigrants respect for higher education.

    You should know these things, Ronald. A more thorough
analysis of your potential market was surely in order. People are
unforgiving. Would you put spurs, a cute little saddle and a
stetson on your pit bull in Calgary-Alberta? You do not break
taboos regarding the communal adhesive in an Italian neighbour-
hood. They will never forgive such a slap in the face.

    "Why do you suppose they quit sending all that scrumptious
pastry?" Wanda asks, her head still lolling backwards. "I could
sure go for something sweet right now." Her hands make small
circles on her ballooning belly. Really. I mean, there ought to be
a law compelling people with bellybuttons like hers to wear a little

black rectangle over the obtrusive thing.

"I am sure that all that ultraviolet radiation is not doing the fetus any good at all." Ronald sees his wife's head whipping up and quickly throws back his own, stretches his legs, folds his arms across his chest and affects nonchalance.

"Ron, will you just shedup! You're so stupid, it's no wonder the neighbours hate you! . . . And he's not a fetus, he's little Terrence." She pouts as she pats herself, then lowers her head until its crown touches the water, arches her back and makes grabbing and hauling motions with her hands, as if she were trying to draw the offending rays towards her belly. A fat angel on the golden rope ladder to heaven. She would bring heaven to earth.

Ronald opens one eye and, satisfied that she's no longer concerned with him, returns to a sitting position and continues stroking his goatee. "Maybe it has something to do with religion, some tribal ritual. You know how closely religious their sort can be. Maybe if I were to scatter a few Ladies of Fatima about the music room, or a nice big Botticelli Madonna and Child up on the piano." He says "Fah-*teem*-ah," and Botticelli like someone in a spaghetti commercial.

"Oh sweetheart, can't we just forget it? It's such a beautiful day, can't you just enjoy it? Let tomorrow take care of itself."

Now*that's* what drives me mad about Wanda Stuart, this let-tomorrow-take-care-of-itself attitude of hers. In the past year I have watched poor Ronald turn grey, literally, in one year. If his goatee is sparse, it's because he is continually pulling at it, as though trying to extract a strand with the solution to his financial dilemma written in teletype: BUY HOLY PICTURES—RELIG-IOUS FUTURES UP. That's the way he does it: he tugs at the thing, loosens a hair, examines it, then tosses it aside disappointed with what he's seen, as though he had read of his own mortality on the contents of a malicious fortune cookie. Perhaps the man had dreamed that by now he would own a chain of music schools and have a student entered in the Moscow competition. Instead of tomorrow taking care of itself, poor Ronald must worry about where his next pool payment is coming from, his wife bovine and luxuriating in her pregnancy, spinning lazily like the black hub of some great wet blue wheel. Still, Wanda is right about one thing: it is a beautiful day.

The sky is as blue as . . . well, as blue can be, and the sun so strong it fights—pours down like honey through the dense needles of the pine tree that partially shades the pool, on Our Lady of the Harbour. Where the evergreen doesn't overhang, the light strikes the water with such brilliance that I have to look away. But the shimmering reflection dances in a rectangular patch on my grey ceiling like a teasing apparition that just won't quit. The corners of my mouth work like the Tin Woodsman's rusted hinges, and it hurts when I am forced to smile scrapingly at the Stuarts and the day. I remember the pitcher of ice-tea I made when I got up, put another cigarette between my lips and head for the kitchen. Perhaps a pine needle will fall precisely, pierce Wanda's tube and send her flailing to the bottom. Go to it, God. You handle the Stuarts, I'll take the earwigs.

Yes, there is nothing like ice-tea for a dehydrated throat smoked drier than Satan's scaly arsehole. Back at the front window, my great Canadian drink in hand, I watch across the street as an old Italian woman walks a little girl, her granddaughter perhaps. The old woman, a black kerchief tied beneath her puckered face, is actually being led by the little girl. A pretty little thing dressed in a yellow crinoline dress, she tugs the old woman along the sidewalk. Once every few steps, she runs to the end of her tether and jerks the old woman ahead. She bends as far forward as she can and looks back between her legs at the upside-down old woman—her grandmother?—and the topsy-turvy world. Perhaps she imagines the old woman a black kite she is flying. . . . But my poet's imagination is not what it should be today. I should have thought new-world tugboat hauling Babushka Barge to her last drydock. And yet, with each snap of the line I feel my heart skip from this taut-wired dance. (What's wrong with me?) I want to take a pair of shears and cut that ugly umbilical. I mean, how often these days does one have to witness a grandmother—great grandmother, for all I know—and grandchild together? There is something frightening in the stark contrast. You'd think we were living in the days of cozy-bunked Noah and crew. So I turn away as they head up the recently poured cement steps. There's nothing wrong with me.

I had heard rumours in the local stinking grocery that a few of the neighbourhood kids were making their First Communions this Sunday. Of course *I* will not be invited to the big party, though I am a Catholic. Not a practising Catholic, mind you, but a closet member of the fold nonetheless.

I drift wearily towards the back room, feeling like I'm wading through maple syrup. I wonder how the Stuarts are making out. A soap opera: has Ronald balded his chin? Has Wanda learned to fear the sun? Will their child be born a new-world mutant, some multi-limbed amphibian, its tentacles crammed into the cookie jar, robbing Ronald of *his* new-world dream of musical immortality? Yes, it is comforting to know that there are people worse off than myself, that there are others with lesser dreams more thoroughly dashed. But as I come up to the window I perceive immediately that something has changed: some issue has been decided in Wanda's favour.

With her belly looking for all creation like a Red Giant about to go Nova, she is laid back and grinning, paddling in circles with one hand and humming—believe it or not—*Ave Maria!* Topped by its protruding belly button, her sunburnt belly twirls like a great pink breast on a black lily pad. What gives? At first I can't see Ronald and crack a painful smile, sip my ice-tea and surmise that Wanda has won some decisive battle. But when I press my cheek to the screen and look down the Stuarts' driveway, I see Ronald standing there with his arms crossed, toeing inadvertently at the driveway gravel. Beside him, talking to him, stands one of the neighbours, his hand resting on the head of a girl dressed in a white crinoline dress, a first communicant, no doubt, as she also wears a white veil.

I try to smile, thinking that Ronald has lost yet another student, and that this is the cause of Wanda's smug joy. But when the little girl twists and runs off, Ronald shouts after her: "Okay now, Francesca, remember, that's Monday after school, four to four-thirty!" And for some inexplicable reason my heart rises into my throat and snags there. But I feel suddenly as though I'm weighted and sinking. I stub out my cigarette, light another, and press my glass of ice-tea to my free cheek.

In the driveway, the Italian neighbour reaches up to undo the top button of his tieless shirt. With one foot he kicks away the gravel and clears a space at the border of Ronald's driveway. He squats down, measures the depth, and with thumb and forefinger held about two inches apart smiles up at Ronald. Ronald nods and merely flicks his goatee. Then Ronald—a surveyor now for God's sake!—steps out the width of his driveway, returns and confers with his neighbour. They nod together. Ronald extends his hand, but his neighbour breaks into a broad grin, reaches out and gently taps Ronald's cheek. Startled, Ronald staggers a bit and actually laughs out loud. And boy what a laugh. Like his poor diesel rabbit turning over in the dead of winter.

Halfway down the driveway the neighbour turns and shouts for all the world to hear: "Omina bring over the boys this afternoon ane-a-we exactly measure you needs!"

Ronald looks worried: "My knees? Whatever for?"

The neighbour flaps a hand at him: "You *needs*."

Ronald looks no more in the know than before: "Ah well. In any case have your boys bring their trunks."

Now it is the neighbours turn: "Trunks?"

"Their bathing attire," Ronald laughs, gripping his thighs by way of explication.

"Ah, a tire!" the neighbour nods, still puzzled. "So we all float in-a-you pool. . . . Like you wife!"

"No-no," Ronald shakes his head, smiling away like the neighbourhood idiot. "We swim," and, seized by some sort of fit, he mimes the Australian crawl.

"Yes-yes, omina do that," the neighbour grins, waves, and Australian crawls his way across the street.

Ronald pulls his T-shirt over his head as he walks back to the pool. He stands ruffling the plentiful hair on his weak chest and grinning mindlessly at the perfect sky. When he looks at his drifting, humming wife, an expression washes across his face like the sun running down a green field. And for the first time since I started spying on the Stuarts a year ago, I feel uncomfortable, inferior to those on whom I had counted for reassurance of my aloof superiority. My cigarette burns my finger and I bang my head against the bottom of the raised window; as I reach for the knocked spot the window drops on my neck and my head is caught fast between screen and window. Ronald looks toward the noise, laughs and waves. Wanda shades her eyes in my direction and squints, her free hand tugging up the bathing suit top that had slipped revealingly low.

Affecting the resonance of an Italian baritone, Ronald sings out, "Santa Loo-chee-ee-ah," runs shouting "A piano student!" and plunges beneath that great revolving breast

I extract myself from the pillory. I draw the blinds, snuffing the shimmering apparition. I miss it. I lick my lips, dying of thirst, but I've lost my taste for ice-tea. I could drive alone up to the lake for the day with a case of Molson's. A swim and a few beers is the only palliative that I've ever found for a hangover. (I *will* quit drinking, tomorrow.) Or I could toss my rough thesis into Lake Huron from the cliffs of Kettle Point, rent a beach shack, and begin a novel: *Under the Sand Dunes*. Ah, but forward revolves the luminous sweephand of my wristwatch. Another lost weekend, lost opportunity . . . and I'm so tired of knocking. Perhaps I will simply go downstairs and pay next month's rent, though it's not due for a few days yet. Perhaps Bacchus—*paterfamilias*, my land-lord—will again offer me a glass of the neighbourhood vino. This time I'll accept. I sure could use a drink. Yes-yes, omina get drunk. There's a cement-a-pour on tap.

Helpmate

Wanda Stuart trudges up the front walk, perplexed as ever over whether Life is cheating her or simply passing her by, or passing her by *and* cheating her. . . . Cheating her *because* passing her by! She stops to look for the absolutely zillionth time at Ronald's sign hanging from the porch roof above the steps:

Ronald Stuart's Academy
of Music
and Art
and Creative Writing

She compresses her lips and slowly shakes her head. She rests a red spike-heeled shoe on the bottom step, cocks back her head and squints at the sign. But it's the noise coming from the living room to her left that holds Wanda: her husband's voice . . . whinnying? Thumping on the floor, squeals of . . . yes, delight! Is that little Terrence squealing? Couldn't be. He'd still be at kindygarten. Her fingers fly to her mouth as though sucked to a vacuum—her own baby's voice she can't be sure of! . . . But isn't that just one more symptom of her stressful dilemma. She nibbles her lower lip and again shakes her head. Why, oh why? Why do *I* have to go out to work while *he* stays home? And just like that the recently roaring, now flagging, fantasy of martinis and supper with her boss (a quiet dinner for two, Brock had winked, three courses) is snuffed by images of blue flames and fondue forks—eating with Ronald by the flames that don't consume.

Wanda focuses the sign and notices that rust has flecked its two chains and embossed lettering. She thinks of Ronald's greying goatee and how in the last few years he has balded a spot under his chin from constantly pulling at his wispy beard, a beard like on an old woman with a hormone imbalance. As though *he* has worries. Well, if the sounds that startle her again from within are proof of what she suddenly suspects, she will indeed give him something to worry about.

That sign will be the first to go, she determines. No more illusions. She simply must remove Ronald's blinkers and show him the straight and narrow. Look what *she* had sacrificed today: an intrigue, an affair, a... What was that word she'd read the other night? ... Yes, a *liaison*. Oh, maybe there's still some hope—a flicker, she smiles—with Brock. But put that on a back burner, Wanda honey, something's just gotta be done with Ronald now.

And Wanda prides herself on decisiveness. After all, it was she who had decided after Terrence's birth that they must move out west to Calgary-Alberta and all that oil money. Ronald's Academy of Music had failed like a bad dye in London after the new music school had opened. "Musica Italia," the competition's sign had proclaimed, and Ronald's accordion players had answered the call, one by one, then wave upon wave. "I'm being squeezed out," Ronald had joked, too often, the greying goatee hairs coming away like . . . well, like grey facial hairs in his effeminate fingers. In a compromise they had moved to Sarnia. Not exactly the wild west, but at least a mini oil boom had been occurring in the Chemical Valley, the refineries desperately upgrading facilities to handle heavy crude.

Wanda again compresses her lips and slowly shakes her head. *Four years.* I'm not getting any younger. She sets down the small bag of groceries, smooths her dress and twists her neck to see her non-existent hips. Though *some* men still find me attractive enough. So what if the gals in my books are barely out of their teens? I'm a youngish thirtyish, and I'll never grow stout.

Ronald had brought his sign along from London. After the initial success of his music school downtown, he had moved the business into his home, eventually adding Art, then Creative Writing, to his curriculum. And why not? As Wanda had argued, hadn't he thrown good money after bad taking night courses in both things at Lambton College? She had prodded him to diversify, quick to lay the blame for failure on his limited skills and mismanagement, afraid he would remember that she was the one who'd finagled him into moving the successful business into their home. As if a real successful man would let a woman force him to do anything. But of course he'd failed, Wanda smirks at the sign. Ronald's a born failure.

"*Crude* is the word, all right, for these herdsmen of the Valley of Chemicals," Ronald complained when his students were gone. "Crude and hea-ea-vy," he would add, frequently attempting to humour Wanda as she hurriedly left for work. But his twitty British accent ruined the whole joke. "Ah well, as your good friend Dr. D'Arcy informed me the other day, among school children Sarnia has an incidence of pre-frontal epilepsy that makes the Love Canal look like Mommy's edenic womb itself."

"Huh?" Wanda had said.

She should turn around, head for the nearest phone and call Brock. Reliving in imagination the way Brock had towered over her at the water cooler that afternoon, Wanda shivers and hugs herself. She steals to the side of the sheer-curtained window and composes herself for a look. Are her worst suspicions about to be confirmed? She can only fear, hope, a whirlpool of emotions lashing her like a warm winter wind.

And today of all days! She'd gotten off early. Her intuition had told her she was making *un grand* mistake even as she'd turned down her employer's suggestive invitation to a quiet dinner for two, three courses. Instead, she had planned a fondue, just she and

Ronald alone together, bickering over the colour-coded forks. And now this. Ronald fondling another woman!... *Sex.* She might have known. It's all he ever thinks about.

"What's a *fon*due?" Ronald never fails to ask as he skewers the cube of sirloin.

"Huh?" Wanda questions, dropping her puzzled look with her lower jaw as she realizes she has again fallen for his sick joke.

"Fuck a buck!" Ronald howls, loudly using the F-word.

"You call that a joke."

Which usually goads him into making fun of her books with his other joke about Sir Loin, some title with the word "tenderizer" in it. Then he has to explain that it makes fun of some writer and his crazy wife, *F* Scott-fits-somebody, as if I'm so stupid as to believe that somebody would have the name *F*. Then he doesn't know to shut up and leave even a bad joke, but goes on and on and making up some whole new stupid story every time about Fondue and Sir Loin.

How *could* she have missed seeing this coming? Blinded by convention, she determines. That's what I am, a blind woman. At least this finally explains the dirty questions he started asking about my books eight months ago.

"Yes, but exactly *how* tall?" Ronald had pressed for details, lying beside her in bed, his right hand behind his head, his left remembering the cigarettes she no longer tolerated.

Wanda rested her open paperback on her chest, sort of like a butterfly (the book): "Oh, I'd say about six feet. But that's not the most important thing."

"And, dare I ask, what is?"

"Oh, I don't exactly know. It's hard to put your finger on."

"It *what* to put your *what* on, Wanda?" Ronald whispered in mock-shock. He took her hand and pulled it towards his thigh.

Wanda shook him off. "Oh Ron," she drawled. "But he's always tall and dark and—"

"A big bucking black man, Wanda?"

"I was gonna say handsome . . . shorty. Though *Cosmo* says

there ain't nothin' wrong with black men neither. In fa-act . . ." Wand squirmed: "Ronnie?"

"*Ronald*, dear. And I do wish you would watch that affected twang." Ronald snapped his words like a stick along icicles.

"Oh, sure, all right, sure thing, *hon*," she drawled even more. "And I s'pose if I jawed like bloody Mary Queen of Scotch the kids would just be a-clamberin' at the windows for bagpipe lessons. . . *loser*."

"Forgive me, love."

Wanda raised her paperback.

"But tell me, sweetheart," he again interrupted. "Are the heroines always destitute and tenaciously virginal, or have they, too, become more, uh, *liberated?*"

"Well, yeah, sort of . . . Huh?"

"Wanda, one cannot be a *sort-of* virgin.. Present company excepted, naturally."

"Yeah, but she's always just about ready to drop her linen for the guy, 'specially if he'd only see he's madly in *love* with her."

"Yes, I begin to see. And they still live happily ever after?"

"Course, dummy."

Ronald had pondered this information for a few days. Another night he'd placed a hand on Wanda's thigh.

"No, Ronald," she whined as she pushed his hand away. "I'm just at the good part."

"No-no, I only wanted to know: these romances, are they permitted to excite you . . . sexually?"

"*Ron-ald!*"

"All right, all right, my dear, I have my answer. Just one more query: approximately what portion of the action is given over to the chase, what comprises the dénouement?"

"For *Jeezuz* sake, Ronald." She pulled a handful of the paperbacks from the bedhead bookshelf and, in her helpful way, dumped them in his lap. "There, read 'em for yourself, *queery*."

To her surprise Ronald had read them, and more, till he'd exhausted her store. He began bringing a few home with the groceries, staying up half the night reading and, to Wanda's enduring perplexity, taking notes on the unused yellow pads of legal paper she'd bought in quantity from her teacher while taking the para-legal course at Lambton College. (After which course, she'd decided to become a lawyer. So? What she was, a legal secretary, was almost as good). Eventually his interest in her books reached the point where he was writing more than he was reading. Impulsively (that quality Wanda had developed in herself and admired most after her considered decisiveness), she once tried to snatch the yellow pad from his hands.

"Now-now, dear," he cautioned, restraining her with his left arm, the pad held out over the floor in his right.

"Jeezuz, Ronald, what in tarnation are you doing there?" She had acted vicious, but as Ronald only smiled with a strange and defiant confidence, she sat back pouting. "You're writing tales about me and my books for that asshole D'Arcy, that's what you're doing. I know it. Just like you told him lies before."

"*Sweetheart?*" Ronald was genuinely hurt and concerned. "Dr. D'Arcy knows, you know, and I know. We *all* know how well you are now. Did he not explain it to both of us together: post-partum depression, the stress of the move, your obsession with that old Joanne Woodward movie, et cetera, et cetera?"

But as she continued to pout with her chin on her breast bone, her lower lip turned out largely, he relented further. "Okay then, listen." He flipped back all the pages and read:

The last late leaves of Indian Summer lay strewn about the grounds of the manor like myriad drops of sunlight. The light that danced shimmering through the leaves of the winnowed willow bejewelled the fish pond with gems of promise. And light danced in her aquamarine eyes, sparkling hope, an iridescence of love's promise. Had not the Master smiled an haughty smile when she was introduced as the new mechanic? Had he not snorted with agreeable equine aplomb? And when he clasped his cane and thumped towards his cellar study, had he not nodded his stern approval to Turk the housekeeper? He had, all of those things.

She frowned at the blowfish that darted about the leaf-strewn pool like . . . like . . . Oh, like lots of things! she reflected. The fish, like her thoughts at any rate, circled the stone column that broke the surface of the water and rose straight up to terminate in a welcome bulbous bath for her late-leaving chums of the air. She tapped the greasy calipers in the palm of her soiled left hand and gave rein to her presumption, vent to her misgivings, air to her secret. Oh, but the Master's limp was ever so slight, becoming really in its thickly mysterious way, unremarkable but for the knobbed cane that drew one's attention to it constantly. And he had acquired his wound saving his unfaithful wife, the gorgeous Gurlavine, from a stampede of big horses at the plowing match in Lucan. Besides, the slight limp detracted not at all from his erect stature, six-foot-plus. When her eyes had shifted to the left slightly, to the head of the cane, she had realized with a start how strong those veined hands must be, a sheetmetal worker's hands. . . . But what was she thinking? She was a dreamer, a dreamer, mistaking disdainful courtesy for more than her lowly position as manor mechanic could possibly promise for the future. Even if she is the first woman to assume such a position at Sadely Manor.

"What's her name? What's his name?" Wanda asked. "Is he married still? How'd he hurt his leg again? . . . Where'd you copy that from anyway? I don't remember that."

"Patience, my one love. I do not yet know their names. But do you like it?"

"Can I have it when you're finished?"

Ronald held his goatee gently: "I think he is going to be a descendant of the Marquis de Sade. Thus, Sadely Manor."

"The what?"

"Oh, just a Frenchman who lived once upon a time, a greater lover of your sex?"

"My *what*, Mister?"

"Very sorry, sir," Ronald snapped like a soldier.

"But you mean this is another one you're making up as you go along, and this time you're *writing* it down?"

"Well, yes, dear, trying. Of course, I've revised this piece some."

"Does she get him in the end?"

"So to speak. You should know that, dear. But first she must convert him."

"Of course, but what from?"

"Patience, dear."

"Read more, *please?*" Without waiting for an answer, she dropped her book, tucked herself in and squirmed comfortably.

"All right. But just a little more. It's all I have finished anyway." And he read:

Yes, she felt herself fortunate indeed to have such a position of responsibility thrust upon her. But what could her position portend. Love? ... Ah, she was indeed a dreamer, again dreaming of rescue as she once had when left alone so often in the Bluewater Orphanage hard by the Chemical Valley. Rescue, yes, but in a relationship of equality.

She plunked down on the rough stone of the fish pond and trailed her middle finger in the dirty water. As if in response to her longings, a blowfish swam up to her finger and hovered there, its tiny cheeks inflating and deflating like those of some tiny submerged Dizzy Gillespie. Little musical kisses blown from another world. Perhaps, she sighed inwardly. If only, she thought mentally.

But what of those sounds she had heard last night, her first night at the manor out on Lakeshore Road? The high-pitched whine of machinery, and a noise like a big-bitted drill. As though someone were trying to drill his way up through her bedroom floor right beside the escritoire that stole her leisure hours. Not an unpleasant sound, mind you, more like the ratchet call of . . .? And there remained the gorgeous Gurlavine, a jetsetting concert pianist and celebrated designer of livery. Still, the Master had asked her to tune the Ferrari. . . . Oh, she was surely dreaming again, she chastised herself, slapping herself hard on the cheek. She soothed the cheek: But then, are we not all dreamers? Do not some dreams come true for some sometimes? We are. Some do.

"What in tarnation are ya saying *rat shit* call for? You shouldn't use that kinda language in a love story."

"Go to sleep, Wanda."

"Read more."

"Be patient, dear. At present there is no more."

She had been patient, for six months now. Ronald had stopped writing in bed. He'd bought a typewriter and arranged a makeshift study in the basement, where he spent his days and nights tapping away. The yellow pads are locked in a chest, which he shoves under the basement steps, away in among the cobwebs so that Wanda wouldn't dare try to reach it. And secretive? The only word of his work is his continual complaint that he can't think of names for his hero and heroine.

"How about Lance and Cynthia?" Wanda once suggested at breakfast.

"Lucy and Peanuts," Terrence chimed in.

"Loose penis?" Ronald winked at his son: "Watch it doesn't fall off."

"*Ron-ald!*"

Terrence's eyes bugged slowly. He jumped and had the fastener to his pants undone before Wanda caught him.

"That'll be enough of that, young man," she scolded, looking meanly at Ronald. "Take your lunch and wait on the porch for Ms. Baird. Go on now."

She stared hard at Ronald: "And what, tell me, is wrong with Lance and Cynthia?"

Ronald relaxed with a surprised snort. "*Cynthia*," he all but spat. "Not delayed gratification, *sweetheart*. None at all!"

"Huh?"

"Not romance and rebirth, *love*. *Still*birth."

"Wha—"

"It's a parody, dear, a highly ironized romance. But I want to be able to sneak it through the proper channels. Harlequin or Cupid. One of our great Canadian abortion houses."

"You mean, it's not for real?"

"Good grief."

"Ronald, you can't do nothin' right."

Shaking his head Ronald had descended into the basement. Thus had ended Wanda's familiar connection to what she sarcastically and loudly referred to as "the *work* in progress." She had returned to her own paperbacks, and had soon found herself fantasizing more vividly than ever about Brock.

One Sunday morning she had walked into the living room and found Ronald, who had not been to bed at all the night before, lying on his stomach watching a TV cartoon, with Terrence sitting crosslegged by his head. Ronald held a book closed on a forefinger marking his place near the end.

"Pamela," Wanda read the title aloud, curious, as it was too big a book physically to be one of her romances.

Terrence and Ronald glanced behind and returned to the TV. Terrence's mouth was smeared with chocolate. Ronald's eyes were red, swollen, and three-quarters closed.

"Or virtue rewarded," he mumbled without turning. "The edifying epistles of Samuel Richardson, the granddaddy of delayed—"

"*Ron-ald!* How could you let him eat chocolate goop first thing in the morning?"

Ronald waved her off with the book: "Sh-sh, it's chocolate milk, he had toast with peanut butter and honey."

"Oh . . . Well how was I to know!" But as no one paid her any heed, she held her chin and watched the cartoon.

On the screen a skunk leisurely bounced along after what was obviously a cat, though a frantic cat that had somehow acquired a white stripe down its back. The cat, its eyes bulging, its whiskers galvanized, clawed over fences, tore through garbage cans, left a cut-out of itself in a tree trunk, but could not put any distance between itself and the patient skunk. The skunk hopped nonchalantly along, sure of his goal, a tiny blue beret tilted at a rakish angle on his head and a little red ascot around his neck. A close-up of his eyes displayed two throbbing hearts for pupils. He paused, clasped his paws at his left shoulder and spoke, in English, but with a sonorous French accent of the kind that had made

Maurice Chevalier the big screen's grand authority on coquettish love. *"Cherie,"* he called to the alley-trapped cat, "I know we must play these *petit* games of love—*ah oui, les jeux d'amour*—but you are tiring out your Pepe." Tiny paws held supinely, he moved in, an embossed heart straining at his chest. The cat clawed air and zipped over the fence, gravity be damned. The skunk winked at the camera, shrugged, and hopped onward.

Ronald grabbed Terrence's forearm: "What's his name?" he demanded, in an accent not quite so British as was his yawning answer to Wanda.

"That's Pepe," Terrence laughed, startled only at his Dad's ignorance. "Pepe le Phew!" Terrence held his nose and spoke nasally: "He always thinks that the boy cat is a girl skunk just 'cause it walks under some paint and gets a white stripe."

"Pepe!" Ronald shouted.

"Le Phew!" Terrence shouted just as he was knocked over by his father and wrestled about on the carpet. "Play horse!" Terrence managed to squeal through his giggles.

Wanda had shaken her head and left the room; a real woman with a real woman's needs, she needed a real man in the worst way.

On the porch, with her left hand touching her lips as though she would restrain herself, Wanda inches her head forward. The living room is strewn with pillows and cushions from the couch. There's Ronald flat on his back, wearing only a housecoat and his burgundy socks with the diamond pattern. His legs are so repulsively thin and white and hairy like . . . like pipe cleaners! Brock back from an afternoon of raquet ball, a real pipe in his teeth, was like . . . something else. Ronald lies spread-eagled on his back with a leather belt strapped around his chest, panting, his cheeks dimpled by the . . . the satiated smile that reminds Wanda of better times.

"Come on, buckaroo," Ronald shouts, clapping and rubbing his hands. "Think you can take me, let's go, I'm up for more." He sits up, turns over and positions himself on all fours. "Yee-haa!" he screeches and begins pumping his hips.

Wanda squints to see through the sheer curtains and the tears she knows will soon be gathering at their saline source. But she will not make a scene. Definitely not. If Ronald is driven this low, to such animality, she will not intrude. She'll quietly retrieve her groceries and leave. Perhaps it's not too late to phone Mr. Anderson. *Brock,* she reminds herself, closes her eyes and sees his thick, waving, and just-that-right-touch-of-grey hair, like that Frenchman who advertises the dye on TV. A mature man. She recalls the time she'd caught him staring when she swung up from the bottom file drawer, the appreciative journey of his eyes up her long thin torso, her broad flat chest, her thin face with its pinched cheekbones, to meet her challenging aquamarine eyes. A model, that's what she'd've been if not for Ronald and his dreams of cultural gold mines. How Brock had insisted that she simply must see the new house he'd built out on Lakeshore. "Oh, we don't need to bother the workaholic," he'd winked when she suggested they'd come out some weekend. And it's only a certain kind of man who can wink without looking dim-witted. Then that twinkle in his eyes, the promise of a quiet dinner for two, three courses. In French no less. And now this!

She compresses her lips and again peeks through the window. Ronald is still pumping his hips and, yes, there, he did it again, actually kicking up his heels once in a while.

"Sweetheart," he calls, "will you flush the bloody thing and hurry on back." He rests on all fours, his chest heaving, his forehead nearly touching the white pile. "And only one more ride. I'm utterly tuckered."

The F-word! Again she compresses her lips and chastises herself. Well, she would not refuse Brock again. And now she could say yes with a clear conscience. Yes! she would say. Or, Yes, oh yes! . . . Still, there is something vaguely attractive, something erotically riveting in this revelation of Ronald as sexual tiger. Had he really been working all those nights? She is struck again by the injustice of it all. She *will* turn around and walk away right now. But not quietly. Oh no. She'll *stomp* across the porch, *pound* down the steps, *tear* along Front Street. . . . Yet something holds her still, a tickle in her throat that snakes downward like a hairline crack opening, closing, breathing to life. She thinks she hears a rumble from somewhere deep down, a guttural "Ohhhhhh."

"All right, love," Ronald calls. "I'm counting to ten. If you're not back by then, I'm taking off the belt. One . . ."

A belt! How could he? She slaves for him. She'd tolerated his criticisms of her, even as she'd watched his students laugh at him behind his back. And it *was* him they were snickering at, no matter what Ronald had insinuated. Okay, maybe at one time she had wanted to go back to work. But that was years ago, two. Ronald seemed to enjoy going off to work in the dining room, so Wanda wanted that life, to go off to work, naturally. Ronald stayed out of the dining room and took care of Terrence while Wanda worked, which began to seem a pretty cushy arrangement for Ronald. How was she to have known of the deadening work most women were still doing, until she *experienced* it? Or if Ronald was right when he argued that ninety percent of *people* wouldn't work unless they had to, or they were convinced they had to. "And you don't have to, sweetheart! We've got oodles from your daddy's trust."

"But women today need a definition of themselves as other than wife and mother. And so do I."

"*What?* They need *what*, Wanda? Look, sweetheart, let's not confuse the issue. People talk that crap because capitalism now makes two incomes necessary to maintain a lifestyle once supported by one—*that's* fucking capitalism—"

"Ronald!"

"Doesn't it strike you as coincidental that it becomes fashionable for women to work *outside the home* again just when one average income will no longer support the North-American family in the manner to which it has been led to grow accustomed, let alone buy the prized cocoon."

"Huh? . . . Oh, trust you, ya bum, to turn the whole issue away from women's rights and the problem of child-care."

But work outside the home soon grew boring, then tedious, so Wanda wanted to be be chief care-giver to her own offspring.

What could be more natural? When she sat down with a pencil and figured out their savings and interest income versus expenses, she saw that Ronald *was* right. She was not so small as not to admit when he was right. And in the meantime *Cosmopolitan* had been softening its attitude towards red lipstick and the housewife; househusbandry was out, cocooning was in; traditional lifestyles were back, Wanda was away all day! Life was passing her by and cheating her at every turn.

Well, this is the last straw: a daytime orgy hosted by her own unemployed husband, to which his own wife has not been invited! And why? Because she works during the day. Wanda decides then and there that she will phone Brock this very instant. Perhaps she can bring herself to resign over drinks. But she cannot move a foot, not yet, not till she's at least seen her husband's partner in debauchery. She squints to see through her faint reflection on the window.

Poor Wanda. That's the way she likes to think of it, as debauchery, as orgy, though she's never before thought of an orgy in relation to Ronald. Ronald is an ogre, imprisoning her in a sexless marriage, yet exposing her daily to the temptations of adultery. (Old-fashioned word, she smirks at her image, shows my age, but maybe it's coming back too.) Oh, she knows his type too well, there's an ogre in every book she reads, the enemy of romance, the embodiment of tendencies Wanda calls "animalistic." Isn't Ronald always spoiling her bedtime reading—her *one* peaceful moment in a hectic day—with his animalistic tendencies? His filthy and nowadays inky hands pawing at her alabaster . . .

The pathetic truth is that poor Wanda Stuart is a compulsive, often malicious, liar, a resourceful liar to and about anyone who happens to graze the filaments of her life, and though a liar mostly to Ronald, an artful liar capable in moments that arrive less rarely these days of attaining to the gifted liar's heaven and deceiving even herself. In short, Wanda is the real thing that her employer, the lawyer Brocklin Anderson, carelessly calls his simply devious, red-handed client as soon as he's out the door: a bullshit artist.

Wanda lies without cause and often without effect, save the pleasure the aesthete derives from having totally invented and completely controlled a fabrication she can abandon at will. The sad truth is that poor Wanda is incapable of telling the truth. Perhaps it bores and scares her, with its mundane predictability and abstract authority. Unfortunately, though, her more inspired, or vindictive, artifices are not wasted upon Ronald. He trusts unquestioningly his wife's honesty in the face of a world out to get her.

If a new female acquaintance is introduced into the Stuart household, Wanda soon complains to Ronald of the battery of slights she'd suffered whenever he left the room. This new woman is after Ronald, Wanda lies to herself, convinced that no woman in her right mind would want such a wimp. And accomplished character assassin? Ronald resignedly has to terminate all developing friendships with other men, shocked and hurt that such ostensibly decent chaps would wink and paw at his wife as soon as he turned his back. He had to agree with Wanda: Yes, most men are animals underneath. To *think*, he had barely been out of the room when his latest golfing partner began leering animalistically and using the F-word in a way that left no doubt of his intentions. But Wanda said it was best not to think about it too much.

With consummate skill, Wanda had almost manipulated Ronald into closing his music school even earlier than he had. But his own initial success had buoyed his resolve to stay where he was. And it was this perseverance that had inspired Wanda to the creation of what was, if not her most elaborate ruse—because the, as she had labelled it, "ersatz" breakdown could not be forgotten—at least her most prolonged and productive.

When they had first moved to Sarnia from London, Ronald had rented one of the small stores still left on Front Street. Concentrating then on music, he had managed within a few months to attract thirty students. In the early stages he had to give all his time to business. And business boomed with the influx of upwardly-mobile engineers and technicians into the Chemical Valley. As many piano students as accordion! A violinist! But despite his early success, Ronald had to close up shop just when his clientele had surpassed his goal of forty students. Wanda had begun to complain of obscene phone calls, of receiving them.

As with all her fabrications, there was a basis of incontestable fact to this complaint. The phone had indeed rang a number of times in the months Ronald worked away from home. Wanda had indeed picked it up and given her best breathy *hello;* there was indeed what Wanda still describes as a "pregnant pause"; the caller did indeed hang up. Just like that. *Nolo contendre.* Wanda insisted to Ronald that she was subjected to such trial all day and evening. And why shouldn't she? The animalistic pervert's calls would surely reach that frequency if something wasn't done! There was, of course, no way for Ronald to investigate her tale. A call to Bell revealed that it would cost thirty dollars simply to have a man come out and look at the disarming piece. So Ronald had their number changed, then unlisted, but to no avail.

"They're too smart for you, Ronald!" she shrieked, perfect hysteria, the first night Ronald came home after having had the number unlisted.

Yes. The suggestive calls continued. Once, when he had stayed downtown till way past five, five-thirty-something, Ronald had returned home to find an authentically trembling Wanda dressed in her housecoat and sitting in twilight at the dining-room table, staring dead ahead, a carving knife in her clenched white fist, her hair in rollers, an apparently untouched magazine by her nail file. Dark strangers had been lurking about the windows (passing on the sidewalk, and out of sight so quickly that Wanda's neck kinked), banging on the front door and rattling the knob (the paperboy was owed for five weeks). Ronald was surprised, alarmed, and totally sympathetic.

"It is a busy street, dear," he comforted, prying the knife from her hand and almost knocking over the open bottle of black nail polish. He went into the kitchen to put the knife away. As he was returning the wine and cheese to the fridge, a thought—other than that he would like some wine and cheese, or anything—struck him and he called, "This city *does* seem to have more than its fair share of Jehovah's Witnesses."

"What's all that got to do with it! That don't matter squat to animals! They know when *you're* not home!" A woman teetering over the abyss of desperation.

"Yes-yes, honey, I noticed that. Always when I'm not home." Ronald was genuinely concerned, Wanda shook so. He attempted levity: "If I were a detective, by Jove, I'd suspect it was *me* causing you the trouble."

But Wanda was having none of that. "Ronald, this is not funny. I'm going mad." She shivered more violently. "See?" she said tremolo, holding out a hand that fluttered like a flag of burnt skin on a windy beach. Then for a moment her eyes glazed over and she wasn't there.

"Gadzooks, but they must be a clever lot. And it *is* a team, I suspect. I keep such odd hours, they must watch the house round the clock. But how does little Terrence take it?"

Her child's name brought her back: "Oh Ronald, how would I know? For Jeezuz sake, he's just a baby. He thinks it's some sorta game." Wanda's head snapped involuntarily. She stared blankly.

"There, *there*, honey." He patted her head, the force of her honest fright having chased whatever doubt lingered. He would do whatever she wanted. "What do you want me to do?"

". . . a game." Wanda snapped out of it. "Of course, he's just a child. He can't know what today's woman suffers in her life!" She managed the perfect pitch of welling hysteria. "Like *you*, you . . ."

"There, there, love."

"Ronald?" she whined with a cagey, petulant submissiveness, her lower lip trembling. "Couldn't you move the school—I mean the *academy*—here, like you had it in London? Just for a little while, *please*? Then you can do what you want with your life. You've got enough students now." She sobbed.

After a few such scenes, Ronald had moved his business home. The students who followed soon grew weary of Wanda's requests to be helped with every household chore and her demands to be driven everywhere. When the roll of students had dwindled to ten names, Wanda began complaining that she couldn't hear herself think when the baby was napping, what with all the scraping of violins, banging of pianos, and crushing of accordions. A little boy no longer, Terrence had suddenly reached the age (three) when he could—when for his own good he must— attend daycare. Having been comparably healthy since birth, he was way behind kids whose immune systems had been incessantly tested and fortified in a viral Dieppe.

"It'll help him adjust to kindygarten."

"That's two years away! Surely three is a tad young to begin training as the corporate cog! Even these days!"

"He's probably already a social retard."

"Yes, Wanda, what a three-year-old needs most is mingling skills."

"He'll develop a better sense of himself as a *person*."

"Indeed. Our toddler will be the very India of independent *person*hood."

"Say it don't spray it."

Ronald now had time on his hands anyway. Why couldn't he—why *shouldn't* he—look after Terrence when he wasn't being cared for outside the home. 'Sides, *someone* had to earn some money.

With *Cosmo's* ten tips on re-entering today's challenging job market in her deep-purple-nailed hands, Wanda had strolled into Sarnia's meagre business district wearing a sheer white skirt slit to the hip and a chartreuse blouse opened only to the fourth button. Brock Anderson hired her on sight. Two weeks later he fired the middle-aged corseted woman who'd been his legal secretary for twenty years. After a few months his practice had begun to decline, as had its owner, behaving distractedly, and inappropriately animalistic.

For two years now Wanda has barely managed to keep Brock's hands off her. And such hands. Like the branches of a pine tree in Spring, not at all like Ronald's brittle lily-whites. So? Everything connected to Ronald is somehow flawed, deformed:

his failed business, the way he had to twist what had sounded like a perfectly good love story into some kind of sick parroting joke. The pervert. Brock has hands like the hero of Ronald's story, the kind that melt the sheets. She's reached the point where she must either throw herself into those muscular arms or quit. Then whence the mortgage and food money?

"Eight . . ." Ronald's voice sustains the eight for at least fifteen seconds. "Ni-unnnn . . . Sweetheart, if you don't get your wee butt back here right now I'm starting supper."

That's it. The decision's been made for her. He has never *once* started supper for her. No wonder he can skip the meals she zaps for Terrence and herself if he's been spending all his time in the basement planning secret suppers and fucking liaisons—oops. Well, the decision's been made for her, thank the Lordy. She'll phone Brock, accept the inevitable dictates of love. Then tell him that she's quitting work. It is just not meant to be. No. The stars have charted for us else. Either that or demand a humongous raise.

Unwilling to look again through the window, Wanda tiptoes across the porch, steps softly down, and retrieves her bag of groceries. She stashes the bag in the bush at the end of the front walk. The Sara Lee can keep or go to the devil for all she cares. In fact, come to think of it, she's not at all sure she'll be home tonight. She strolls smartly along the sidewalk, continually flicking her hair back off her shoulder, like Mary Tyler Moore when she played attractive women. She can see the phone booth. *Who can turn the world on with a smile . . . Ciao,* little miss goody-two shoes, Ms. perfect homemaker-breadwinner. *I can bring home the bacon, fry it up in the pan . . . Bonjour,* debauchery!

In ten minutes Wanda is back, poking distractedly through the bush, tearing at the leaves, breaking through the branches. If she were in her right mind, she would think of the tiny green leaves that lie strewn about her feet as so many feathery emeralds. But she's in no condition for fantasizing. Her hair sticks every which way from the mussing she administered while on the phone and from the twigs that penetrate it. Her mascara streaks to either side of her mouth like a clown's tear tracks. Poor Wanda. And here she'd always pictured a hesitant glycerin droplet in matters of the disappointed heart, droplets to be dabbed at, not smeared with the back of a snotty hand. A drop of blood trickles from where she bites into her lower lip. Frantic, truly touching hysteria, she kicks the soggy plastic bag onto the front walk. She stands straight, touches her hair with rigid fingers that stab through to her scalp, then smooths her dress with such force that the seam tears around the waist.

HOW COULD YOU HAVE BEEN SO STUPID? something screams from somewhere deep inside in a voice that is neither male nor female. She stands stock still, terrified. I, I thought he'd meant a quiet dinner for two, three courses. *AND YOU WITH ALL YOUR READING IN MATTERS OF THE HEART.* A woman, and familiar. Don't laugh at me, you! But that's what she should have yelled at that animal, Mr. Brocklin Anderson. *A quiet dinner for two, three courses*, the voice echoes, definitely a woman's voice, a calm maternal voice, reassuring, yet suggesting a difficult security. The perfect smarmy Mom. *What will you do to me next? Have you no respect for anyone?* But look what he's doing in there, she whines, beginning her pout. I deserve some fun—*NO.* The word flashes through her, up and out the top of her head. She looks up at the bright undersides of the poplar leaves glimmering in the soft wind. Then a chastising whisper: *You know who is in there with your husband.* I don't, honestly, I really ... She feels the darkness inside turn, from side to side like a head shaking, her head, dizziness. Shut up shut up shut up! You're the liar! Bullshit artist! What the hell do you know about women today! She weaves from border to border as she stumbles up the front walk.

What's she doing talking to herself like a goddamned mad-woman? She suddenly feels untouchably alone, and looks for cover. Inside, whatever is going on, her only hope.

Back on the porch, her old self returning seemingly intact, she checks for scratches, assesses damage. No harm done. No fault. One of life's faultless fenderbenders. Nothing she can't smooth over. Temporary insanity, that's what it was. And who wouldn't go a little crazy again, disappointed at every turn as she's been, deceived in ever dream of love and romance? Denied even a decent affair. *Ménage à trois*, Brock had said again on the phone. "Where?" she'd giggled. "In my hot tub, baby," said a breathy Brock, "with Stella, the Mayor's wife, you've met her. Maybe even a foursome off the big tee if Alderman Wain's wife, Lucy, comes along." "Huh?" So Brock had waxed graphically, promising, as she'd witnessed him do with manys the client, more than any man could deliver, she supposed. But it's not her fault the animal had deceived her! It can't be! Who else on God's sacred earth has been so vigilant? And the mortgage! Can she take back her resignation? Maybe if she just— She hears a squeal from inside the house.

"Giddy-up, Daddy," the voice calls. Terrence's voice. Of course. She knew that. She was playing with herself. Inside, go inside.

She stands unnoticed by the archway to the living room, her left hand gripping the metal hook on the uncomfortably mirrored hall stand. Terrence is riding Ronald's rump, his hands gripping the belt strapped around his father's chest. Wanda wants suddenly to join in their fun, desperately, impulsively, but she can't loosen her grip on the hook. Anyway, she would only embarrass herself. She is about to sneak upstairs and fix her face when Terrence is bucked to the floor.

"Mummy!" He runs to her and wraps his arms around her thighs, presses his cheek to her abdomen, then steps back. "Daddy's a star!"

"What?" Her hands flutter up like burning butterflies, touch her hair.

"Honey!" Ronald gasps. "What happened?"

Terrence steps back, alarmed, examining his mother for something he's missed.

Ronald jumps to his feet and steps in front of Terrence. He gently touches her limp arm with his right hand, his left yanking at his goatee.

She commences crying: "I was attacked, sexually, I think." She falls into his arms, trembles, steps back.

"I'll phone the police." Ronald steps toward the kitchen, but she blocks his path.

"It's all right, dear. They didn't r-a-p-e me."

"Pee me," Terrence giggles, cramming his hands into his crotch.

"Little pitchers," Wanda cautions. "Let's not make a big deal, okay? I'm all right, really."

"But what *happened?*" Ronald pulls spidery goatee hairs away in his fingers. His wife is safe nowhere! In broad daylight! . . . And today of all days. "Did you get a look? The p-o-l-i-c-e *should* be informed."

"I see me!" Terrence squeals.

"Ronald, you've already said *po* -lice. But it's all right, it's over, finished, caput, thank God. I got off early and was coming out of that little Italian winery beside the Spectator offices. Someone pulled me into a dark alley that slopes down to the river."

"Good grief! Was there only one?"

"One what?"

Ronald's hands are shaking; to cover, he takes the stub of a pencil and a yellow pad of stickums from his shirt pocket: "One assailant?"

"What are you, the fucking police?"

"Wanda!" Both Ronald and Wanda stare horrified at one another.

"Ronald, I said *no police.*"

"Rest assured, love, there will be no police. Now, just tell your story."

"Huh? . . . Well, he took me from behind, the pig, pressed against me with his big greasy hand over my mouth. He had this real low scary voice, probably disguised. He just breathed down my back and mumbled, with a French accent I think, that he knew us and was going to show me what love is. And he said something about, uh, about getting even with his mother, *all* women."

"Ah, love," sighs Ronald and takes her hand.

"Daddy's gonna be on TV. He's gonna be a *big* star." Terrence shows how big.

"What?" she asks, pushing Terrence's hands away from her face and looking at Ronald.

"How did you get away?"

"Oh, I bit his hand, screamed and wouldn't stop. He gave up on me, and when I'd turned around he'd vanished."

"Good gracious God, love." Ronald squints in thought, nods his admiration, makes a note.

"But what's he talking about?" Wanda is in full control again, she feels, and curious. "Shouldn't he still be at kindygarten?"

"Oh that," and Ronald lets himself grin. "But are you sure you're all right?" He pats her hand.

"Yeah, okay, I'm fine." She throws his hand back at him.

"And you don't think we should phone the hmmm—"

"Ronald! For Jeezuz sake!"

"All right, all right. Come right this way." Taking her by the upper arm in an unfamiliar grip, he turns her and leads her across the hall into what was once the dining room, was then the music room and is now the dining room again. On the table sits a vase of yellow roses.

"Oh," she sings, clapping her hands like blinkers to her temples. "Mine?" she asks coyly.

"Daddy's gonna be on TV!" Terrence shouts, clapping his hands together.

Ronald picks up a half-folded typed letter from beside the vase. "There, read it for yourself, as you once said to me."

She unfolds the letter and reads quickly, mumbling portions aloud and growing more excited with each word: "Dear Ronald Stuart, I am happy to inform you that Cupid Books would like to publish your novel, Pepe and Pam, by Randi S. Stafford, this Fall. . . . very excited at your first effort . . . local colour pleasantly surprising, as is the *new woman* in a contemporary, if somewhat regional—yet traditional—setting. . . . a bit of a departure for us doing a romance in hardcover . . . looking forward to meeting you *and your wife* . . . forthcoming cheque against advance royalties for *five thousand dollars.* . . . a long and mutually rewarding relationship . . . Percy Stingle, editor-in-chief, Cupid Books Inc."

"Stupid books stink!" Terrence shouts. "Daddy's gonna be a big famous star on TV!"

"Oh Ronald!" she gasps; her jaw drops: "TV too!"

"No-no, love," he grins, tugging the tips of his collar and rocking up on tiptoe. "Not yet, in any case. Just pulling the boy's leg. But yes, *Pepe and Pam,* by Randi S. Stafford, a-k-a your loving husband, Ronald Stuart, Esquire."

"What's aykayay?" asks Terrence, and fails to break the spell.

"I can't believe it!" She sets the letter on the table, then doesn't know what to do with her hands. She pinches a petal off a yellow rose.

"They bought it," Ronald leers impishly, rubbing his palms together. "Hook, line and sinker. Head, tail and afterbirth—they think it's for real! And the good part is I've left myself open for an unlimited number of sequels. I'll be whelping romances for the rest of my life! Oh, are our lives ever going to change!"

"What's it *mean?*" cries Terrence, over-excited and upset.

"It means none of your business, now shut up."

"You can quit work!" Ronald proclaims.

"I can quit work."

"I'm quitting school!" Terrence squeals. "We're moving to Hollywood."

Ronald frowns: "I just picked him up early today so we could celebrate our good fortune."

"I'm gonna go phone Br—Mr. Anderson right now and hand in my resignation."

"Do you think that's wise, or at all cricket, love? To leave him in the lurch like that?" But Ronald is now playing with himself. Such a minor concern. It is simple pleasure to flirt with something other than *his* triumph. Already his thoughts have left Wanda and are returning with the consuming lust of an absent lover to his only concern: work, success, more success.

"But it's dangerous down there, Ronald. 'Sides, he's been making passes at me lately. I didn't wanna tell you because we needed the money."

"Down where? . . . Pardon?"

"I'm getting a real horse," Terrence says, serious like his parents.

"I can stay home *all* day. And we can decorate the dining room like a real study. Maybe I can learn to type, and do p-r."

"Pee-are," spurts Terrence.

"The basement? . . . Yes." Ronald comes clear: "I have to go check a few things." He pats Terrence's head and walks absently to the basement door.

"Ronald?"

He turns, his hand on the doorknob: "Hm?"

"Who's Randi S. Stafford? Have you been *working* with someone? Do *I* know her?"

Ronald chuckles to himself. "That, love, is my androgynous *nom de plume*."

"Bomb the moon, bomb the moon!" Terrence continues barking the order through the grimy hand that pinches his nose and covers his mouth. He spreads his free arm like a wing and swoops towards his father at the the opened basement door. But Ronald prevents the lopsided flight downstairs, so Terrence changes course for the living room.

"Huh?" she frowns.

"My pen name, for fuck's sake!" Ronald's eyes pop and he swallows. He descends the steps, the door thudding shut behind him like a vault's.

Wanda whisks Terrence off his feet, plants him on the living-room floor not three feet from the television and turns it on. On her way into the kitchen she stops at the basement door, kisses it, pats it, then opens it. "I'm gonna phone Anderson at home and quit. Okay? . . . Ronald?" There's a rumble from the dark basement. "Ronald?" Then irritated, "Did you hear what I said down there?"

"Will you shut that fucking door!"

She softly shuts the door. Anyway, in mysterious ways, graceful ways, God was still on her side. No doubt about that. Here at long last was her just reward, the big payday. She had caught Life by the scruff of the neck and given it a good shaking. From now on if there was any cheating to be done, *she'd* be the one to do it . . . henceforth (she must learn to speak better, what with the people she'll be meeting). It was the devil who'd baited and berated her only a few moments ago on the front walk. But of course. She can see that now with penetrating clarity. The devil in human guise had deceived her into believing there was real love and romance just beyond the horizon. It was the devil who'd tempted her to despair, to blame herself. And of course he'd pretended to care for her welfare, in a woman's voice no less, that patronizing—*maternalizing*—warm tone of his. Demonic deceptiveness. She'd read of such momentary possessions. Animalistic lust was behind it . Not a true passion, *une affaire de coeur.* Just like the deranged wife, the insanely possessive witch who crushes the full flowering of the divinely natural love between hero and heroine. But with God's help she would withstand—she *had* withstood the temptation to despair. Me and Ronald, and Terrence makes three! She is giddy, then dead serious. Well, she could teach the devil a thing or two.

Playing out her hand, she walks heavily to the kitchen phone. (Surely he could hear *that* down there; if he has any further objections, speak now or forever hold your peace.) But her next step is too heavy. A shiver stabs across the bones of her feet, vibrates up her legs and rakes along her spine to rest like a claw in the back of her head. It begins pinching the knot that has formed in her crown. She picks up the phone and cradles it against her shoulder. Without needing to think about the familiar deception, she depresses the black button with her left thumb and holds it down. She dials violently with her right index finger, nails be damned, her own phone number, just to be safer. She waits the exact time it would take for three rings. The claw in the back of her head opens, reaches out, a rank exfoliation, white-hot nails burning coldly along the sides of her head, pincers embracing her temples from within. Her whole body goes cold, a thick icicle of fear piercing through her torso and out the top of her skull.

"Hello," she shouts for Ronald's benefit. Something exhales hotly in her ear. She hurries, shrill, near shrieking: "Mr. Anderson, this is me, and I just wanted to give you a piece of my mind. First of all—"

WANDA, whispers the voice from her shivering head. She checks to make sure her thumb still depresses the black button, then holds the phone away and looks at it in affronted bewilderment. *WANDA.* But it is not in the phone, and it is not the voice from before. *MINE, WANDA.* Cold, black, breathy, it whispers obscenely.

The Chemical Valley

My eyes open like those of some deceptively still amphibian, and I anxiously taste my sweet moment of normal awakening, savour it. There's the plain overhead light fixture, its circular shadow the only blemish on my eggshell-coloured ceiling; there's the reassuring light fixture above a sword of dust-free sunlight that slices my westerly-facing room diagonally; yes, there indeed is the cool, pale light fixture like the sun seen from a submarine. . . . Sword of sunlight? Afternoon? *Harooga, harooga, dive-dive-dive.* But before I can sink mentally the familiar question comes spinning into consciousness like a barrel water mine—*VAVOOM!* What did I do last night?

And so it begins again.

My right arm cranes across my body, and stubbing sensitive fingertips I paw about for my watch. One-thirty. Once again my expectant Brenda has been slaving away in that stinking Holmes Foundry for . . . six and a half hours? Lord love her. I make dry noises and with tongue tip ream my parched hole of a mouth. I swallow little spittle down a throat as narrow and dry as the space between an itching elephant and its tree. Fire down below! *Whoop-whoop-whoop!* WATER!

The physical pain is a welcome diversion, almost. Into the bathroom, forget remembering, avoid the mirror, philosophize, theorize, close your eyes and make what spit you can. Or just make water.

A pitcher of ice-tea in the fridge bodes well. But what promising foolishness have I committed now to deserve this gift from Bren? Or is it simply the goodwill glow, the aurora borealis of accommodating pregnancy? Do I need a glass? No. To you, my thoughtful love, and to the devil with drunken promises. *Gulp-gulp-gulp-gulp-gulp-gulp. Aaaaa.*

That momentary respite at awakening, familiar to ever drunkard, convinces me that a good part of the hangover *is* in the mind, not merely floating like ragged sewage in the swollen lobes. Aren't there any sober, securely funded psychologists to contend so? That a telling percentage of the pain is guilt over forgotten behaviour of the night before? No? . . . Ah well. As a result of *my* never remembering the last half of the previous night, I scratch at my anxiety anywhere from two to five days afterwards. The duration of psychic self-abuse exists, I suspect, in some ratio to the depth of my blackout and the rate at which stories of misbehaviour filter through from fellow drinkers, and my Brenda. Generally speaking, and generously, I go two days feeling that acquaintances are making faces behind my back, or that strangers glance, look away and, somehow privy to my anxiety and its cause, just perceptibly shake their heads. It's worse if they're primarily Bren's friends or family.

The day after: I usually don't feel too bad. With the alcohol sluggish still in my blood—licking a wound here, lapping a pain there—I experience a kind of drunk's doldrums. Unable yet to smoke, I watch whatever's on afternoon TV (endless rapid-fire gameshows, special two-hour "Love Boats," but no slow soaps), eat a large bag of Bridge Mixture chocolates and drink a big bottle of syrupy Coke. Sugar stoking. Recuperating. The second day delivers my true hangover. I go through two packs of Craven "A" *Speciale douce* in a vain attempt to smoke down the rising rot in my throat. Good God, it's finally happening, my liver and lungs are breaking up, *gulp*, I can taste them! Myself I just manage to keep together downstairs in my basement, away from Bren. She walks heavily overhead and complains loudly about irresponsibility, infantile men, her lot generally. I'm fine on the third day. A regular solar hero I arise from my self-inflicted wound to reassure my steady eyes in the mirror that I will *never* drink again. Such a sure shaving hand, but one of the many perquisites with which sobriety justifiably baits us. Soon Brenda will love me again, or, seeing that this time I'm for real, will talk decently to me at least. I often check the paper for work on that third day and wonder if I ever had any *real* friends. On the fourth day, with a neatly-ruled list of promising phone numbers and addresses (complete with postal codes) on a yellow legal pad within view, I begin an exercise program in my basement: stretch, bend, twist, push-ups, sit-ups, run on the spot for the ol' tickeroo. Ah but the body really is an amazing machine, a finely tuned mechanism that should never be gummed up with filthy beer, an equipoise of equilibrium that should never be upset by stacked brown bottles. And so resilient! Three months from now, at the latest surely, when *I* stop running on the spot so too will this stranger's flesh that has hung its flabby self upon me.

On the fifth day I feel as chipper as Flipper, so well in fact that I begin drinking in mid-afternoon and consume till about three or four in the morning, beer glorious beer, alone or shared with whomever will still tolerate my company, at home or out, makes no difference, I don't remember anyway. On the sixth day, my eyes open like those of some deceptively still amphibian. . . . And so it begins again, and again, and again.

What was that? *Why* do I drink again on the fifth day? C'mere, Curly. Let me fit this claw hammer into your nostrils. Why you . . .

But that day I had a real job interview at the Fiberglass plant. My improved job *prospect* (as Brenda had emphasized the singular) resulted from two weeks of sobriety three months before. I don't know what happened to my pentamerous cycle. I suppose I just opened my frog eyes one bilish second-day-after and saw my life dissipating like the contrail of a jet headed for oblivion, and

panicked, and scared myself straight for a time. Usually when that
sobering vision strikes I have the presence of spirit to go on a back-
to-back bender. So what happened? Who knows. Don't ask such
questions. Remember the handy claw hammer. I had just turned
thirty-five, maybe it was creeping middle-age. Anyway, thank
God it *was* my day after: unbenumbed by leftover alcohol I'd
never have followed through with the interview.

I hesitated with a fourth spoonful of sugar congealing in the
steam above the scalding tea they say helps shrink the brain's
bloated vessels. I smiled, figuring (as I'd figured before, many
times) that I am useless from boozing about six days out of every
ten: the day of drink, the day after, and the day after that. That's
one hundred and fifty-six days a year. Roughly five months. So
why smile? Perhaps because, in this affluent country of ours,
people such as unemployed I can drink heartily and live well. But
oh. My fingers were splotched with old and new cigarette burns,
the indelible exclamation marks of intense, if forgotten, drunken
arguments. Oh, self-immolating burnout! And for all I remember,
someone else may have intentionally burned me. In a minute or so
I would begin to feel last night's bruises. Yes, I am become a
falling-down drunkard. Legions of— A lengthy note on the
fridge's message board:

Honey, don't forget, your interview's at 2:30. I set the alarm
for noon. Hope that's not too early. You were pretty good last
night and quiet. Wear your brown cords but don't plan to wear
your brown shoes. You peed on them again.

Love, Bren

Take something out for supper. Me!!! Not too sick this
morning. Good luck. And don't talk to the interviewer about your
poetry (Oops, sorry).
XXOO

And so it began in earnest: I'd slept through a noon alarm.

A few of my old highschool friends still worked at Fiberglass, owned their own homes, with living rooms that are just for show and formal dining rooms that no one dines in (those who soberly work can live princely!), have growing children. Brenda and I, both in our mid-thirties and university educated (in my case for a good ten years), had recently returned to Sarnia from failures abroad (Toronto), rented and were expecting our first child. I had worked at Fiberglass before, for three months between my fifth and sixth years of university. I had made an unpopular ass of myself with remarks such as, "I don't know *how* you guys can look at a lifetime here!" When the janitor had the courtesy to enquire in heavily accented English what book I had my face in, I would not deign to look up from the swimming clauses of my *Being And Nothingness*. I took twittish affront when one of my fellow workers asked if there was any good—and he clapped his left hand over his right bicep as his right fist poked the air—in Sartre's masterwork. "Yes," sneered I at the uncomprehended page, "but no pictures, Washoe." My nickname that summer was "Beans-n-nuttingness," then simply "Beans." So I got the job, being the only candidate with previous experience.

As I was re-introduced to the noisier parts of Fiberglass I didn't bother searching my bruised memory for literary Names who had laboured honestly. *Though* (I touched my tender part) if back-cover bios are to be credited—and I suddenly saw no reason not to give them their due—every Canadian writer has dabbled for a spell (or under one) at honest manual labour. From greasy-spoon dishwasher to off-shore derek monkey, haven't our own writing jacks all done such poetic fieldwork before soaring to the rarefied realms of belles lettres? Yes? Yes!

By the way, I myself have published a volume of poetry: *The Chemical Valley* (Bluewater Press, 1986). Print run: 300. Copies sold: 34. The Chemical Valley *suite* (as I had envisioned it being called one day) was composed during the three years I wasted waiting vainly for a job teaching English and Dramatic Arts in any highschool. (I have no idea just what "Dramatic Arts" are; the assignment was my punishment for not having a recognized "minor," a second subject to teach.) My book was "published with the generous assistance of the Canada Council," as duly noted in my "Acknowledgements." (Dear, merciful Jesus, stop me before I start tracing an outline of my other private parts on this innocent paper!) A "series," no less (look, I am spitting), of workingman's poems was my *The Chemical Valley*, from a poet manque who had never held a full-time job for longer than a summer's vacation! (Psst. Hey you. C'mere. Yes. You. Come here. Here now, take this leather punch. That's it. Now, see that part there? Right, that's the one, sonny. Now one proficient squeeze, as though you were tagging for tracking a rare species of idiot.)

But to return, as I did, to Fiberglass. Unlike poetry, Fiberglass of Canada has been a boom industry in these latter days of volatile oil costs and government incentives to insulate. Unlike the generously assisting Canada Council, Fiberglass of Canada is not an institution to foster illusions.

I started that night on the graveyard shift, eleven to seven. (You should have seen my would-be conventional Brenda humming about the kitchen as she prepared me a lunch that would have fed a whale. Never mind that she had already put in eight hours that day at the Foundry.) I was assigned to the first of three stations on the third line, the worst line. Three of us waited at station one for the fiberglass blankets to come smoking out of the babelish machinery that made them and along the rolls of the conveyor like prone and pink bellydancers in a siezure: one man to quality check and pat them straight; the second man to remove, stack, and set them in the mechanical compressor; and the third man to bag the blankets, seal the bags and heave them onto the barge-sized wooden carts that were then hauled to the warehouse.

I stood in position two's enclosed space. Because there were two stations after ours, I stacked every third blanket, twenty-one R-7s to a pile; I then slipped my right hand under, thwacked my left on top, squeezed the load, swung it overhead and slammed it into the other robot that clanged and clamped like an automatic shirt folder; the robot then compressed and rammed the product into the monstrous red and white plastic bag fitted over its rear like a dungcatcher for a whale. The second position at a station on the third line is held to be the worst part of the worst job in the worst plant in The Chemical Valley. Such a shower of irritating glass fibers comes to ground in the space between one's wet neck and one's matted collar when one swings the pink load overhead. In the over-one-hundred-degrees-F heat, pores open breathlessly to the invisible itch. For the first thirty minutes I worked in fear that the very next instant I would tear off all my clothes and run around the plant shrieking and scratching till I bled.

The vaguely familiar foreman watched me perform flawlessly for half an hour, smiled and nodded, pursed his lips and marched off tapping his steel pencil on his clipboard. The three of us at station one changed positions. Thank God it was Day One of my drinking cycle. I worked mindlessly, my nose soon stuffed with the glass fibers that were a welcome diversion from my raw throat and tender memory. Though I still craved a green jelly-filled Bridge Mixture, a continuous swallow of Coke.

When the foreman was out of sight a decent time, one of my fellow workers shut down the line.

"Shit man," smiled the bagger, "you really had us moving. Ol' Will-the-Pill was pleased as piss. You work here before?" He was short, with over-the-ears greasy blond hair, pale greyish-blue eyes that danced, but a thin anemic grinner, and jumpy as the smallest in a large family.

"Yeah, about ten years ago. Funny how it comes back." (I usually say "yes," and I never say "funny.")

"No shit," said the other young guy who'd been straightening the blankets at position one of our station. He removed his gloves and loosened his ascot (and I remembered the protectives). He was medium height and chubby, with long greasy brown hair and deep purplish fat wet lips like a small dinghy run aground on his face. So he seemed to pout as he spoke: "You get laid off somewhere?"

They both looked at me in fearful anticipation: *Please,* stranger, no one moves *backwards.*

There are, I recalled, but two topics of conversation in the

lunchroom at Fiberglass: the first of course is sex, graphically
detailed sex; but the close second is getting out of Fiberglass and
moving up to a better job. I was about to answer with a lie when
there was a bang on the metal shell of the station next to ours. The
boys hopped to it. I was left holding one of the plastic bags.

I felt the foreman—Ol' Will-the-Pill?—standing behind me
as I heat-sealed the bag. When I swung around to toss it onto the
pallet he had to sidestep. A pleased smile pinched his pointy face.
I slipped another bag over the outlet and waited for the stacker to
accumulate his twenty-one R-7s. . . . Not such a bad job, one really
tough half-hour spent stacking the blankets every hour and a half;
certainly not as bad as the nightmares I'd suffered during and after
my previous stint would suggest. Sure I could do this for my
coming child for—*gulp*—the rest of my life. (Here, sir. Yes, *you*.
You see that part of my body. Uh-huh. Take it, slide it between the
pincers of this hot-wire bag sealer. That's it, easy does it. Now step
on that pedal. Ahhhh . . .)

The foreman held his chin, stabbed his forefinger at me,
tickled his chin with thumb and forefinger like a teller counting
bills, then broke into a broad grin. His index punctured the air:
"Beans-n-nuttingness!"

"You got 'er Will-the—" I remembered something touchy
about his own nickname and caught myself. Hadn't he been the
foreign janitor when I was here last?

"The poet!" roared Will-the-Pill.

The kid quality-checking the blankets watched us; the kid
stacking spat fiber and glanced when he could; both looked
worried that I was catching it.

Will called for attention: "Hey boys, guess what? Your new
guy's a poet!"

"Easy, Will, easy." But how in hell had he come to be
acquainted with my *The Chemical Valley* (Bluewater Press, 1986)?

Will-the-Pill laughed, slapped my back, and wandered off
pensively tapping his clipboard. The guy with lips like earth-
worms looked at me with a pitying grin, as if Will-the-Pill had
announced that I was emerging from cancer remission. A com-

pressed stack of blankets squeezed from the robot's rear and, finding no plastic bag, blossomed like a pink carnation accelerated by time-lapse photography, slowly ... then *poof*, twenty-one R-7s nuzzling my shins like skinned dolphins. I kicked the mess under the line with the rest of the rejects.

"Stay on your toes, Shakespeare!" shouted someone from behind.

It was Jim Brown, one of the drivers of the small tractors that hauled the loaded carts. Big Jim Brown. A jerk in highschool, a worker on line three when I last worked at Fiberglass, Big Jim was the sort of pain who thought it hilarious to grip your scrotum when your arms were full. Grown fat and hairless, he had a head like a pink onion. But he'd come up some in the world at Fiberlglass, the goof.

"Hey, good to see ya again! How's about a brewski after work?" He glanced about furtively. They all did all the time in that plant, as though they had just done or were about to do something sneaky. He jumped from his driver's seat and loped over.

I slid the stuffed bag from its frame, set it against the sealer, slipped on an empty bag, sealed the full one and turned with it just in time to ram the groping Brown in the chest. "Forget it, Brown, I remember."

He laughed his laugh like Elmer Fudd's and returned to his tractor. "Finally joined the human zoo, eh?"

"Gotta work, Big Jim." I glanced past him and furrowed as though having spotted the foreman.

He snapped his hands on the steering wheel. "Will-the-Pill likes your stuff. Nice goin'."

Not such a bad guy. "Hey, maybe some other time on the brew."

He shifted gears: "Better hope he doesn't remember you're the one hung the nickname on him. Kraut's like an elephant." He snapped all the fingers of his right hand, slapped the top of his left fist, grinned and drove off. Prick.

But yes. Will-the-Pill. He had been the janitor ten years ago.

A recent immigrant then, with a thick German accent I'd detected
no trace of when he'd just spoken to me. Yes. The Pill. In the
lunchroom once he'd been lured by his malicious coworkers into
a conversation about birth control. Eager to ingratiate himself
with his intolerant new countrymen, and all else having failed,
Will had tried self-deprecation, ignorant of how truly alien such a
stance was to Sarnians, whose dominant style of social intercourse
is an adolescent attack as relentless and tenacious as sharks in a
feeding frenzy. But to my amazement Will hooked and played
those idiots like a native Sarnian (no wonder he's now foreman).
He told in what could only have been purposely exaggerated
Germano-English how he and his wife had "wented on the kin-
derkontrollinkpillses," and how she'd still become pregnant. "But
mine knockerjugs having growned and tenderized."

Someone asked the obvious question: "Villhelm, old buddy,
you don't mean to say *you've* been eating the pills?"

"What!" gasped Will. He slapped his sunken cheek: "My
Sabina is the one who is to be takink the pillses? Uh-oh." He rolled
his eyes like a stage Negro's and smacked his forehead with the
scant meat of his palm. The men roared and rapped the table with
their knuckles as they did to signal "pass" in their euchre games.
A few slapped Will's back and touched his shoulder. He beamed
at the blows.

I stood, crumpled my fiber-infested sandwich in its wax
paper and stared disgustedly at Will. "Will-the-Pill," I sneered
then grinned about at the men.

They howled and kept repeating "Will-the-Pill." Will looked
at me as I imagine *el Duce* stared at pictures of *der Furher* when he
realized the jig she was up.

Will's nickname stuck and my own was used less frequently.
Only Will-the-Pill continued to call me the full Beans-n-nutting-
ness, in clearly enunciated English, for the remainder of that
summer. The other men began dropping the n-nuttingness, my
reward for the joke on Will. Will brushed up a cloud of dusty fiber
whenever he swept near me. In the lunchroom he no longer
removed the covers from what I had assumed were Harlequin

Romances. He sat alternately frowning and nodding at the pages of his Rilke. His book was a parallel text edition, with the German and English on facing pages, and he read it as though watching a tennis match. That week I composed my long lyric, "Will of the Working Ones." See *The Chemical Valley* (Bluewater Press, 1986), pp. 32-35. *Cf.* any poem by Gerard Manly Hopkins, from which my stressfully alliterative sprung doggerel is so shamelessly and incompetently stolen. (See also—Oh, Madam? Yes, you. Would you be so *kind* as to fetch that carpet hammer. Yes, the one that looks like a woodpecker's head, that's it, thank you, do bring it over here, please. And yes, it *is* difficult to speak while keeping one's head elevated, being spread-eagled and all, and in such a state of dishabille. So kind of you to remark my discomfort. But let's not beat about the bush, as it were. I have a small favour to ask of you. . . .)

Before the summer was over, Will-the-Pill was halfway through *Moby Dick*. Nevertheless, his knowledge of nuanced English failed him when Big Jim Brown slapped the book from his hands and with a kick sent it skiing along the floor to catch in the sticky spill and butts at the foot of the pop machine, then asked, "Uh, Willy-boy, what's big and pink and drags on the ocean floor?"

Will retrieved his book, smiling all the while as he wiped it on his white shirt, perhaps pleased at the new form of address: "It is a riddle, *Big* Jim?"

"It's Moby's *dick*, you stupid Kraut! No wonder you Krauts lost the war!" Big Jim slapped his knee and doubled over at the ancient joke.

"The war? . . . Oh, yah, yah, *big* Moby Dick." Will shut the book on his thumb, compressed his thin lips and peered at his paperback, whose cover showed Gregory Peck in a stovepipe hat riding a white whale into the deep blue yonder. He smiled up at Big Jim, then made a serious face: "You know, *Big* Jim, it is perhaps best book I've read, including Mann, who is, ah . . . who is too subjectivity."

Big Jim looked at the other men, shot a mock-perplexed glance sideways at Will and, feigning concealment, pointed at Will from behind his left palm: "What *is* the word on this goof?"

As I was putting my Sartre into my lunch bucket, convinced that Hazel E. Barnes was an inept translator, I remarked offhandedly to Will, "It's only impressive when you're at sea in the middle of it, uh, Will."

"You be offing yourself, Beans-n-nuttingness!" he raged inappropriately.

I was still worrying about Big Jim's reminder of Will's elephantine way with a grudge when I spotted Will-the-Pill standing half-hidden behind the corner of my packing robot. He stood hugging his clipboard to his chest, his head bowed, thin dry lips pursed as though he was, old maintenance man, tidying his thoughts. He looked up, saw me watching and began a smile which soon contracted to a puzzled squint that seemed slightly forced for threatening effect. I had decided to walk into the front office and quit, salvage my pride.

Walking towards me he shouted, "Break time, boys! Shut 'er down!"

In five seconds the line was down and unmanned. As was I. Fixed like a snake-charmed bunny.

He came up to me, smiling through clenched teeth, struggling to conceal the whole range of Teutonic vengeance. He was a short muscular man, though I'd remembered him as even shorter, and not so muscular.

"Beans," he grinned. "You know, it took me *five years* to live down that name you hung on me." His small hand skimmed the surface of his greasy backcombed black hair. Like Big Jim, he'd grown a forehead.

"Uh, Will, did you actually *read* The Chemical Valley?"

"*Five years*," said Will.

"Uh, you remember the poem, Will of the Working Ones?"

"I remember everything! A stupid poem, I wouldn't even call it a poem! I remember, too, what you did to me *right here*." He pointed at the all-too-scant space of floor between us.